Incorporating Your Business

D0836172

Incorporating Your Business

By JOHN KIRK
with the editors of
The Professional Report

CONTEMPORARY
BOOKS, INC.
CHICAGO ▪ NEW YORK

CONTENTS

Incorporating Your Business

1.
Incorporating Your Firm: Its Advantages and Drawbacks

Perhaps you have been thinking about incorporating your business. Or perhaps you plan to go into business for the first time and are debating whether the corporate route is the one you should follow.

In any event, you would like to know more about the ins-and-outs of incorporating. What is the good? What is the bad? What are the first steps you will need to take?

This book will answer those critical questions, and many more, in a clear, straight-from-the-shoulder manner. It will help you decide whether incorporation is for you now or in the future. And should you decide to incorporate, it will guide you as you take the necessary legal steps.

Incorporating a business is not as difficult as you might imagine. You will discover that as you read these pages and gain the knowledge you need.

You will not be alone as you start your incorporation actions. Hundreds of thousands of owners of businesses and professional practices are doing the same thing this year—more than 300,000, in fact. They are incorporating for many of the reasons spelled out in the following pages.

Virtually every large business enterprise is incorporated. Almost all companies that gross $100,000 a year or more incorporate sooner or later. Successful professional persons also incorporate in growing numbers. A 1973 study shows that 63 percent of physicians in private practice who earn $90,000 a year or more have incorporated. In contrast, only four percent of doctors earning under $30,000 a year have done so.

You can see, then, that the more your sales and earnings grow, the more likely it is that you will be incorporating your business.

Basic Features of Corporations

Here is what lies ahead should you choose to incorporate:

• Your corporation, once formed, will be a legal "being" that can sue, be sued, and enter into contracts just as you can do as an individual today. It can be a permanent entity that will not automatically dissolve when you die.

• Your corporation will issue shares of stock which represent the shareholders' right to share in its surplus profits via the vehicle called dividends. And should it one day be dissolved purposely, its shareholders—actually its owners—will have the right to split the money left in the treasury after corporate debts have been paid and to raise still more money by selling the corporation's inventory, machinery and real estate.

• You may choose any name you please for your corporation —provided that the name doesn't conflict with one already in use and doesn't violate a few other considerations to be discussed later.

• When you are incorporated, you will receive a charter from your state which spells out what your corporation may and may not do. That charter will give the corporation's name and address, state its purpose for existence (to make lamps, manufacture garden supplies), and spell out the amount and classes of its capital stock.

• To actually incorporate, you will probably want a lawyer who specializes in such work. (In most states you can set up a corporation without a lawyer's help, but it is not advisable.) Your tax adviser and accountant also can be a great help to you during the incorporating procedure.

• Finally, when your corporation has been established and made ready for business, and you continue with the work you have been doing, you will become its employee as well as being its owner.

WHAT INCORPORATING MEANS

To help you decide whether incorporation at this moment is best for you, let's examine what this step involves.

To start, let's appraise its drawbacks:

● Creating a corporation calls for considerable time, effort, and expense. Once formed, it is subject to much more control and more exacting compliance with regulations than a sole proprietorship or partnership. You cannot run a corporation in the freewheeling way in which you may be running your sole proprietorship. You must have board meetings, annual meetings, reports to stockholders and the like. This continuing, exacting legal compliance by your board of directors and management requires records covering many of the actions of these two groups.

● It could cost you at least $1,000 a year more to do business as a corporation. That is chiefly because you will probably need the continuing services of an accountant and lawyer.

● You will have the additional expenses of setting up a new entity. You must tell the world that you are now a corporation. That may mean changing signs, stationery, telephone listings, and so on if you have previously been operating as a sole proprietorship or partnership.

● As an employee of your corporation, you should live under an employment agreement that specifies in detail which expenses you will be reimbursed for and which you will pay yourself. The contract should also spell out your salary and the mechanism for changing it.

● You will have federal and state governments looking over your shoulder, primarily to make sure they get their full share of taxes. You will have to comply with regulations concerning how much you pay yourself, how much cash your corporation accumulates, and similar matters.

● You will probably have to pay a regular fee to your state—a franchise tax for the privilege of operating as a corporation.

● Your overall Social Security tax will be higher. As a sole proprietor, you contribute on a percentage basis roughly 70 percent of the combined amount you must contribute first as the employee of your corporation and then as the employer. The corporation is permitted to deduct this payment on its tax return, so that the effective tax bite will be less, but your total out-of-pocket Social Security expense will be higher than when you are self-employed. The extra payments you must make will bring you no extra benefits when you retire.

● You will have to pay an unemployment tax to the state and federal governments covering yourself as an employee.

● You may face extra complications when you do business in states other than the one in which you are incorporated. Before your corporation can operate a branch in another state, it will have to file a copy of its charter with that state. In addition, it will have to designate an agent to represent it in each outside state it files in, in case it is sued one day in that jurisdiction.

● If your earnings from your sole proprietorship or partnership are low, there may be no financial advantage to incorporating. What, for example, will the availability of fantastic fringe benefits and profit-sharing plans actually do for you, if your corporation, once organized, cannot afford to fund them?

Advantages of Incorporating

Before you allow yourself to be turned off by the drawbacks, consider these advantages of incorporating. You may find that they greatly outweigh the disadvantages.

● When you incorporate and continue to contribute your services, you become an employee of the corporation and can establish tax-sheltered pension, profit-sharing and bonus plans that pile up deferred income for you. You can also get life insurance, hospitalization insurance, health and accident insurance, lump-sum death benefits and various other fringes whose cost the corporation pays. The corporate form makes it possible for you to realize better wealth-building fringes than you could ever receive via a sole proprietorship or partnership. As a sole proprietor or partner, you cannot participate in employee benefits. As an owner-employee, you may do so.

● Once your corporation is formed, you and your stockholders may no longer have a personal responsibility for corporation debts. That freedom from liability is best appreciated when you consider what happens to the sole proprietor or partner when his business fails completely. His personal assets—home, savings, etc.—may be up for grabs as irate creditors file suits to collect their money.

Such is not the case for owner-executives protected by the corporate form. Under usual circumstances, nobody can touch your personal belongings—not even plaintiffs in cases brought against the corporation.

● When you incorporate, you may deduct the reasonable salary you pay yourself as an employee of the corporation no matter how small the corporation's profit thus becomes—even if profits disappear.

● You may reduce your overall tax bill because two taxpayers share your income. Take the case of an unincorporated business owner whose present income puts him in a 50 percent tax bracket. He incorporates and takes a lower salary so that his corporation will show a profit of $25,000—all of it now taxed at 17 percent. (He may face a personal tax when he seeks to withdraw those after-tax profits from his corporation but, as we shall see, there are many ways to get tax-free benefits paid for out of the corporation's income.)

● Incorporating may enable you to reduce your personal income tax in other ways as well. By taking business deductions wherever possible for medical and hospital insurance and bills, charitable contributions, etc., you reduce the amount you spend personally on such deductible items. But you are entitled to a standard deduction on a personal return regardless of the amount of your actual deductions. If your corporation takes as many deductions as possible, you may be able to take a standard deduction on your personal return for much more than you have actually spent.

● Your corporation can have a permanency not possible with a sole proprietorship or partnership. When a sole proprietor or a partner dies, the business is dissolved and must be reorganized if it is to continue. But the death of any officer or stockholder in no way terminates a corporation.

● Your corporation offers greater inducements for raising capital and borrowing money than other ways of owning a business. Other things being equal, corporate shares can be more readily sold than an interest in a similar but unincorporated business.

● Finally, should you ever wish to sell your business, lock, stock and barrel, you can do it easily without dissolving the corporation. And your profits could be taxed at low capital-gains rates.

Corporations Can Have Privacy

How about the fears of some business owners that incorporating spells instant disclosure of business secrets to stockholders and directors? This is a fallacy. You can incorporate and keep your business to yourself.

Consider this: Most American corporations have no more than three directors—the minimum demanded in almost all states. And those three directors are the husband, the wife, and their lawyer. (In Delaware, only one director is required; and he/she can be the president, secretary and treasurer too.)

As for the fear of too much stockholder knowledge of your affairs, you can be the corporation's only stockholder if you wish. Or you can make your wife and children stockholders along with you. In any event, stock ownership in your corporation need not go beyond your family.

2.
Five Basic Reasons
Why It Pays to Incorporate

It is a fact that more than 300,000 owners of businesses and professional practices choose the corporate format every year and that large businesses, almost without exception, are incorporated. In itself, this says a great deal about the advantages of operating as a corporation instead of a sole proprietorship or partnership.

Let's examine in detail why a third of a million entrepreneurs incorporate their firms every year. There are five primary reasons.

Fringe Benefits Are Fabulous

In the main, you can get more fringe benefits as an employee of your corporation than via either of the other forms of business ownership. However, whatever fringe benefits you provide for yourself you must provide in the same proportion for anyone who works for you and meets certain basic requirements as to length of service, etc.

Here are the benefits awaiting anyone who embarks on the corporate route:

● You can institute a plan that will let you put aside huge chunks of cash that won't be taxed until retirement when lower tax brackets will probably prevail.

As an employee, you can be included in your firm's profit-sharing and pension plans—even if you are the only employee. Those plans are more liberal than comparable plans that can be established by the self-employed.

For example, a sole proprietor or partner may set aside up to 15 percent of his net earnings per year. (Net earnings are what you have after business expenses are deducted from gross income.) He may deduct a maximum of $7,500 per year. As the employee of your own corporation, however, you will be able to deposit in a qualified pension and profit-sharing plan 25 percent of your yearly compensation or $25,000 a year, whichever is less. This amount may be in the form of profit-sharing or stock-buying plans or pension fund, and may consist of contributions made by your firm as your employer and yourself as an individual.

Annual payments you can get upon retirement under a pension plan may reach as high as $75,000. Lesser payments may not be more than the average amount received in your three best earning years. Say you earned $35,000, $40,000 and $45,000 in your three best years. Your annual pension payment may be as high as $40,000.

● You can get "free" health insurance—the entire cost deducted as a business expense by your corporation. As an employee, you now become eligible for the various group health plans that can financially protect you against medical, hospital, surgical and dental expenses, loss of income due to disability, accidental death or dismemberment. Six kinds of coverages are widely sold:

Hospital expense insurance. This pays the costs associated with hospital confinement, including room and board, routine services, use of operating room and drugs and medicines. Under some plans, a flat dollar allowance is provided for maternity care, but most plans pay virtually all hospital costs. Emergency out-patient care is generally paid for as well.

Surgical expense insurance. This covers surgeons' fees up to stated amounts. Most contracts contain a schedule of the maximum amounts to be paid for specific surgical procedures.

Physicians' expense insurance. Under some plans, benefits are paid for a specific number of doctors' visits in the hospital up to a maximum dollar amount. Some plans cover patients' visits to the doctor's office or doctors' visits to the home.

Major medical expense insurance. Also known as catastrophe insurance, this protects policy-holders against medical, surgical or hospital costs that could otherwise be ruinous. A typical policy calls for the insured to pay a certain amount (perhaps $100) before the company pays anything.

Accidental death-and-dismemberment insurance. This provides special benefits if an employee is killed or suffers the loss of limbs, sight, etc., in an accident.

Disability income insurance. This helps to replace earnings lost because of absence due to accident or illness.

• You can get a term life insurance policy with a face amount of up to $50,000—the premiums also deducted by your corporation as long as the policy does not name the corporation as your beneficiary.

To be tax-deductible, the insurance must be group-term. This is protection for a fixed period of time provided under a master policy or a group of individual term policies. You must include all employees in this benefit provided they meet certain reasonable and consistent standards—for example, after they are in your employ for three months. Coverage must be made available to all employees according to the same ground rules.

• You can set up an insurance program that provides reduced coverage for retired employees, including yourself of course. You might buy coverage that declines in steps after retirement to half of the pre-retirement coverage and then remains in force for life.

• You can also provide group life insurance for immediate members of your own and other employees' families. Most policies of this kind are rarely for more than a few thousand dollars per person. Some policies give wives or husbands of employees (but not children) the right to convert to permanent insurance if an employee's job ends for any reason—in your case, if you sold or otherwise disposed of your corporation.

• You can pay a $5,000 tax-free death benefit to the beneficiary of an employee—including your own beneficiary if you die.

• You can exclude from your taxable income the dollar value of any meals or lodging furnished to you by your corporation for that corporation's convenience.

You Escape Personal Liability

A single proprietor is personally liable for all debts of his business—even if he must sell his home to pay off creditors. As a single owner he cannot shirk his liability.

The same condition faces a member of a partnership: no shirking of responsibility. Worse yet, each member of a partnership is liable not only for his or her actions but is also liable for the actions of all other partners.

For example, if your partner incurs a debt on behalf of the partnership, it becomes your debt as well. If another partner or partners cause a libel suit, you may be sued along with the person or persons responsible for the litigation.

Such painful drawbacks do not exist when you own a corporation. That means that, under ordinary circumstances, once you have paid for your stock you are no longer liable for the acts of the corporation. Nor—again under ordinary circumstances—are you liable to creditors of the corporation; your losses are limited to money you have invested in the corporation. Further, you are not personally liable for unauthorized acts of your employees.

This avoidance of liability on your part does not mean your corporation cannot be sued. Nor does it mean that you can go scot free if your corporation goes bankrupt and your creditors can prove misrepresentation or fraud on your part or show that you siphoned off most of its assets for your own benefit. In that case, you will become personally liable even though you have been protected by the corporate shell. The law will not allow out-and-out fraud to go unchecked.

Here is one attempt that was uncovered and punished. A man set up an inexpensive textile business with himself as the only employee. He bought on credit thousands of dollars worth of goods in the name of his corporation, sold the goods at a handsome profit, then took most of the corporation's income as his salary, leaving nickels and dimes in the treasury to pay the corporation's bills. When creditors took the man into court, the judge held him personally responsible for the debts. The court ruled that the man had deliberately set up the firm to rob his suppliers.

Ordinarily, when a corporation goes bankrupt because of the bad luck or bad judgment of its owner, the stockholder or stockholders cannot be held personally responsible. In fact, the law allows the owner of a corporation which goes bankrupt not only to walk away from it but also to set up another corporation the next day.

This ability to escape personal liability is especially important to business owners who, while operating a relatively small enterprise, are nonetheless forced to buy sizeable amounts of merchandise or supplies. Such businessmen run the risk of having a bad season that can put them out of business. And should that happen they may have unpaid debts running into the thousands.

Liability protection is also desirable for anyone whose business by its nature puts the owner in constant jeopardy. For example, publishers of newspapers, newsletters, and magazines are always targets for libel suits that can run into the hundreds of thousands of dollars.

Another aspect of liability lies in a different area posing its own unique problems. That area is product responsibility.

Product responsibility concerns damages to property and injury incurred while the product you made or sold was used by another person, usually your customer or an agent of the customer. (An injury may also occur while your product is merely dormant on the property of the customer. Such cases may involve explosions or fire and water damage.)

A few examples of product liability:

• An electrical device you manufacture severely shocks and burns the consumer, sending her to the hospital for emergency treatment and later confining her to her home for several weeks.

• A consumer's child dies from lead poisoning brought on by the child's munching on the paint you or an employee (or a machine) applied to one of your products.

• A product you make or sell falls apart while being carried from one room to another by your customer and breaks his foot, ending his ability to earn a living for several months.

There may be situations where carelessness, or deliberately substituting lower grade materials, or inferior workmanship, or the failure to inspect according to government regulations and requirements, might make you liable personally. In most cases, however, when goods or services you make or sell cause loss or injury to your consumers, it is your corporation that is responsible, not you as an individual.

Tax Breaks Are Bigger and Better

In enabling you to minimize taxes, the corporation stands head and shoulders above the other forms of ownership. Incorporating brings with it tax benefits unknown to partnerships and sole owners. It also brings some tax disadvantages, but these can be made fairly harmless.

Here are the major tax breaks corporations and their owners get:

• You start with a clean slate when you incorporate. Your new corporation is actually a new taxpayer—just born, so to speak. And thus you can choose the corporation's fiscal period—in effect, ending your tax year when it best serves your interests. You are not hemmed into the conventional calendar year. You may also choose various accounting methods that best suit your needs.

• You avoid questions concerning your right to deduct losses.

Individuals who own unincorporated firms can deduct losses in full only if they were incurred in trade or business or in transactions entered into for profit, or if they were casualty losses. In sharp contrast, corporations are not so restricted. The I.R.S. assumes that all corporate losses are incident to the business of the corporation.

● You can spread ownership of your corporation among different members of your family. Through the medium of stock certificates, you can transfer assets to your children without hitting them with a heavy tax burden. Here is how that is accomplished:

Your children get their shares free. Over the years, they collect dividends generated by their shares. Because they are children, chances are great that they have little or no other income and consequently are in a low tax category—if indeed they are taxed at all. That means that the dividends they get are relatively undiluted by taxes.

This technique also protects you against the possibility of keeping too much cash in your corporate treasury, making it subject to accumulated earnings taxes. (For a full discussion of accumulated earnings, see page 84.)

By giving shares to your children—and your spouse, too—you give them an interest in your business which may allow them to continue to control it upon your death.

● You can dictate the year in which you and the other shareholders (if there are any) will receive their dividends. You control the dividends. And that permits you to distribute stockholder income over a long period to give yourself the most favorable tax treatment.

● You gain estate-planning benefits. For example, it is easier to give away shares of your corporation during your lifetime than it would be to give away a piece of a partnership into which you had entered. And when it comes to bequests, your corporation can continue undisturbed even though new owners now hold a controlling interest. (Partnerships and sole proprietorships would have to be reshaped into new firms.)

● When you sell your corporation, you can arrange the sale so that profits are taxed at the low capital-gains rate. By including retained profits in the assets you sell, you may pay a lower tax on them than if you had distributed them to yourself as dividends.

What about the so-called tax disadvantages?

To begin, while earnings via the corporate route are taxed twice, the corporation's tax bite will not be severe for most individuals launching a new business venture. That is because those start-up years generally are years of low income. Moreover, it is relatively easy for you, the corporate owner, to lower your profits with a solid salary and sensible spending—both of which are legitimate business expenses and deductible on your corporate tax return.

Is it possible that the double tax is not the villain you thought? Consider this: The corporate tax bite is 17 percent on the first $25,000 of taxable income; 20 percent on the next $25,000; 30 percent of the next $25,000, and 40 percent on income between $75,000 and $100,000. Bear in mind that the profit figure is arrived at by subtracting from gross sales all salaries, rents and other expenses. For many business owners, corporate tax rates — at least on the first $50,000 or $100,000 of income — are lower than the personal rates they presently pay.

Your corporation—if it is typical—in the early years will not earn $50,000 or more, at which point the tax rate is 30 percent. Thus, you can probably count on paying the low 17 or 20 percent rate for some time.

Obviously, if you have been avoiding incorporating because your earnings will be taxed twice, you may have been making a decision based on an invalid assumption.

Furthermore, there are legitimate ways to cut down on the taxes your corporation must pay.

• Pay yourself a generous salary. Take out of the business as much as you can without setting yourself up for high personal income taxes. You must follow a careful line on this. If your salary is extraordinarily high, the I.R.S. may insist that you lower it. (The I.R.S. is well aware that a high salary spells lower corporate profits and lower tax revenues for them.)

When I.R.S. agents look at your salary to determine whether or not it is "reasonable," they use the following yardsticks:

Your background, training, abilities.

Your corporation's sales and earnings.

Your direct contribution to corporate earnings.

The I.R.S. probably would not mind if you paid yourself $50,000 a year—provided owners and executives of other firms your size in your industry earn that much or more. But if the I.R.S. can prove that not one executive in your field (in a firm as large or as small as yours) draws more than $25,000 a year, you may have a tax problem on your hands.

Certainly it often makes sense to shoot for the highest salary you can legitimately take, because the higher your salary the lower the profits on which your corporation will be taxed.

There are many ways you can draw a salary the I.R.S. considers reasonable and still legally take home many more dollars than appear on your pay check. Such devices include owning the building you rent to your corporation, leasing equipment to it, and loading up on the tax-free fringe benefits mentioned earlier that would otherwise be paid for out of your personal pocket.

• Use year-end tax planning techniques. Almost every corporation owner can save substantially by using them. Your income and business expenses will doubtless vary from year to year. If your income is exceptionally high in one year, your tax rate (and the percentage of taxes for each dollar of your income) is also likely to be exceptionally high. On the other hand, you can arrange matters so that your taxable income isn't unusually high in one year and thus you can keep your tax rate down. Spreading taxable income from year to year is the usual way of achieving this. You can do it in two ways: deferring income so that it shows up on next year's return instead of this year's, and stepping up payment of your expenses so that you show a lower profit this year.

Full details on how to use year-to-year planning to cut taxes will be described in the chapter on tax strategy.

• Use investment tax credits intelligently. Tax-wise managers know how these credits (allowed by the government when you buy most kinds of business equipment) can slice their tax liability. If you buy an item that qualifies fully for the credit you can cut your tax bill by up to 10 percent of its cost.

You may deduct the amount of the credit from the total tax due on your return and you take the credit for the year in which you place the equipment in service. Sharp managers anticipate their needs and take delivery before the end of a tax year in order to get an immediate tax reduction.

There's a limit to the total credit you can take—ordinarily, not more than the amount of your tax liability for the year. But that reduces your tax bill to zero—nothing to complain about.

• Revalue inventories and write off bad debts. Businessmen who offer goods for sale generally have some dog-eared, outdated or otherwise inferior merchandise which is not worth the price they paid for it. By writing down the value of such inventories at yearend, you reduce your profit and therefore your tax. You will have to offer the goods for sale within 30 days after your valuation date, sell them for scrap or dispose of them as trash.

To take deductions for bad debts, you must establish that you have made all reasonable efforts to collect. The regulations require you to take the deduction for the year in which the debt becomes worthless. However, you have in your own hands the power to speed up or slow down your collection efforts and also—to some extent—to determine when there is no longer hope of collecting what is owed you.

The fact that there *are* ways to keep corporate taxes low is proved by the findings of researchers for Merrill Lynch, Pierce, Fenner and Smith that hundreds of the country's largest corporations pay less than top tax rates.

These corporations theoretically pay a tax of 48 percent on each dollar of earnings above $50,000. But one in four corporations studied paid less than that amount. One company, American Express, had an effective tax rate in 1973 of only 18.5 percent.

Large corporations operating across national boundaries have a few special ways of cutting their tax rates. For example, those operating abroad get tax breaks in the U.S. on earnings they retain overseas. But most ways of reducing tax rates are available to corporations of every size. Viewed in this light, the double taxation you encounter when you incorporate becomes less menacing than it might first seem.

Money Is Easier to Raise

If you believe that you will have to raise sizeable sums of capital over the years to finance various ventures as your business expands, you have a sound reason to incorporate.

It is easier for a corporation to raise money than for a comparably-sized proprietorship or partnership. The reason hinges on the fact that corporations—unlike the other methods of doing business—can sell shares to virtual strangers. And those shares represent ownership in the corporation.

Investors so like the idea of buying shares that many investment companies specializing in lending money to small businesses will not consider applications from anyone but corporations.

Since it might be possible for a stranger or strangers to buy sufficient shares to call the tune in your corporation, you will probably want to make certain that at all times you (or you plus your wife and children) hold enough outstanding shares to enable you to maintain control.

It's Easier to Transfer Ownership

Corporations can live forever; corporate owners cannot. Thus, when you—the corporate owner—die, ownership passes to your survivors and your business can continue without interruption.

To fully appreciate this ease-of-transferral advantage, consider the situation of a man or woman who dies while a sole proprietor or the member of a partnership. Often the business comes to a screeching halt while an administrator or an executor takes immediate control of the assets. At such a time, it is even possible for government authorities to impound bank accounts and other assets necessary for the conduct of the business. Such actions are taken so the government is assured that all inheritance taxes are paid.

It is true that the administrator in such circumstances can post a bond guaranteeing the payment of inheritance and other taxes and allowing the business to continue as usual. But the red tape and expense necessary to carry out that plan are considerable.

The corporate form could make it much easier for your business to survive without you. Ownership in a corporation rests with its stockholders in proportion to the number of shares they hold. If one survivor inherits enough shares to exercise effective control, he (or she) can proceed much as if he inherited a sole proprietorship. He will be able to decide whether to keep the business going or dispose of it.

Usually he can make the decision stick regardless of what the minority stockholders think. It is true that minority stockholders (those holding less than 50 percent of the shares as a group) could cause plenty of trouble for management. They have a right to vote, can demand all kinds of details about the company's affairs, and can sue the controlling stockholders for alleged failure to safeguard their interests. Nevertheless, control of the firm is clear-cut.

Besides making the corporation more manageable, keeping a substantial block of stock in few hands can have important estate tax advantages. The Internal Revenue code provides for significant tax breaks for the heirs of a person whose stock in a closely-held corporation comprises more than 35 percent of his estate's total value at the time of his death.

3.
The Incorporation Process, Step by Step

Assume you have decided to incorporate an existing business—a sole proprietorship or a partnership—or a venture you are about to launch. What steps are involved? Can you take them on your own? Do you need a lawyer to help you?

To answer the lawyer question first:

It is easier to drop the whole business into the lap of an efficient, competent attorney than it is to handle the chore yourself.

But along with the pleasant handing over of the details to a lawyer is the necessity of having to pay him a fee.

How big or small a fee depends on: where you live; whether the lawyer belongs to a prestigious firm; whether you are a big businessman known to be wealthy; whether the corporation you are starting is limited to one state, or is a large organization that will operate on a regional or national basis.

Small legal fees typically (but not always) go hand in hand with non-urban areas, lawyers with a general practice, middle-class owners, and smaller-than-average corporations.

Big fees are usually linked to larger cities, highly regarded law firms, and well-heeled incorporators starting larger-than-usual businesses.

Does that mean the small businessman in a small town using the services of a local lawyer will not get as good a job as his counterpart in a major city? No—provided the local lawyer has had some experience in bringing other firms to incorporation.

Incorporating a business—especially a small one—can be a cut and dried affair. For the most part, the higher legal fees that many businessmen pay are the results of two factors, one economic and the other psychological:

Economically, the bigger law firms have higher overheads, must charge more for services. Psychologically, some businessmen need to feel they are getting the best treatment and soundest legal advice, and only a high fee instills in them such feelings of confidence.

Lawyers are often reluctant to discuss fees on the grounds that no two cases are precisely alike and that their charges are often based on factors which cannot be pinned down in advance. However, one report in 1974, the result of interviews with attorneys in all sections of the country, revealed that average fees for incorporating a small business ranged from $250 to $800. According to this survey, you could expect to pay from $300 to $400 in the northeast, $250 to $350 in the midwest, $250 to $500 in the south, and $500 to $800 in the Pacific Coast states.

It is standard advice to shop for legal fees, but this advice does not make much sense. A lawyer's service is not a standard commodity like a name-brand television set. More important to you than saving a few dollars at this stage is getting someone who can fashion your corporation according to your particular needs and perhaps save you thousands of dollars in the long run. A $500 incorporation by an experienced lawyer who can advise on how to set up your tax year most effectively, will be worth far more than a $200 incorporation by someone who botches the job.

Obviously, the best way to find out how much you will pay is to ask your lawyer. But before you do so, determine if he is the man you should be seeing. Does he have the necessary experience? Or will your case be one of his first in this field?

If he is inexperienced, do not retain him. Instead, telephone your local chapter of the American Bar Association and ask for the names of lawyers in your area who have had extensive experience in setting up corporations.

Thus far this discussion has centered on retaining a lawyer to do the work for you. But the task of incorporating is not impossible for a layman on his own. In most states, you do not need a lawyer to take the steps of incorporating outlined in this chapter. You do not need legal help to clear your proposed corporate name with the Secretary of State or other state official in charge of incorporation. You yourself can obtain and fill out the required forms containing the information that your state will require. "Corporation kits" containing stock certificates, corporate seal and model by-laws are sold to laymen by legal stationers. Even stationery shops which do not carry such items in stock can order them for you. Nor do you need a lawyer to hold organization meetings or meetings of shareholders. This book contains all of the basic information an individual needs to incorporate on his own, and sample by-laws and minutes for the conduct of corporate meetings are contained in the appendix.

Even though you could incorporate on your own, it is generally unwise to bypass legal assistance. Doing it could ultimately cost you much more than the legal fees you save. Here's why:

How you set up your corporation can have highly important tax effects. There are many pitfalls that only an experienced professional can protect you against—and many tax-saving angles he can show you how to use. A qualified lawyer's charges for setting up a small business corporation are seldom more than the firm can afford, but the potential savings which his services make possible could amount to thousands of dollars.

Another factor to consider is the value of your time. It doubtless will take you much longer to go through the incorporation procedure than it would take the experienced lawyer who has been through all this many times before. Presumably, you will be taking time from your regular work and cutting your own income in the process.

SEVEN STEPS TO INCORPORATION

Whichever route you take—hiring a lawyer or doing the job yourself—you will do well to know what is involved. With that in mind, here is a detailed explanation of what must be done to incorporate your firm.

Step 1—Choose your state of incorporation.

Before you file a piece of paper—or even see a lawyer—you should decide which state will become your state of incorporation.

That requirement may come as a surprise. Indeed, you may have believed you had no alternative. You may have assumed you had to incorporate in your home state.

This is not so. You may incorporate in any state you choose.

That does not mean that if you lived in Ohio and chose New York as your state of incorporation that you would have to do business in New York. On the contrary, you could do all of your business in your home state and continue to be a New York corporation.

Why would you want to incorporate in a "foreign" state—a state other than the one in which you do business?

The reason is a solid one: The right to charter a corporation is vested in the state. Along with the state's right goes the power to impose reasonable regulations on any corporation incorporated within its borders. And some states have stricter regulations than others.

Obviously, if you seek to operate in the most free-wheeling way possible, you might wish to incorporate in a state less demanding than your own, one more friendly to businessmen and their corporations. Your state might require more directors on your board than you prefer. It might insist that a certain number of directors be residents of the state of incorporation. Or it might require a larger dollar investment in your corporation than you had planned.

Each state has its own ideas on how owners of businesses and professional practices may and may not incorporate within its boundaries. In most instances, the differences among states are almost invisible. But in a few cases the differences are vast.

Some time ago the American Bar Association devised a "universal" set of rules, hoping that every state would adopt them, thereby making incorporation in California the same as in New York. That set of rules is formally called the *Model Business Corporation Act of the American Bar Association.* Almost everyone speaks of it as the Model Act.

Many states over the past few years have adopted the Model Act, making incorporating more standardized. Some have adopted some provisions of the act.

The surest and quickest way to find out where your state stands is to ask. Most states publish information concerning incorporating procedures, fees, etc. It is often available free, but some charge nominal fees for the booklets they provide. You probably can get the specific information you need by writing the Secretary of State of your state at your state capital. (Information on specific state regulations and fees is not included in this book because they are constantly changing.)

It is generally agreed that if you plan to operate your corporation interstate and thus take on a national character—with intentions of going public in the future—you might do best to skip your home state and incorporate in a friendlier state like Delaware or Nevada, which have made an industry out of the business of incorporating. They work at attracting enterprises to their borders the way other states strive to lure tourists to their woods or beaches. Nevada in its advertising stresses that it has no income tax (personal or corporate), no franchise tax, no inheritance tax, no estate tax, no gift tax, and no transfer tax on capital stock sales. Delaware will allow one incorporator to start a corporation and be its only stockholder.

However, if your enterprise is relatively small and you are not thinking of operating interstate, you will do better to incorporate in your home state even if it has relatively strict regulations. Here's why:

Say you do your business entirely in Nebraska but have incorporated in Delaware. Your home state will look upon your Delaware corporation as a foreign one, requiring approval before it may be admitted to do business in Nebraska. To get that approval, you must go through a costly procedure much the same as if you were seeking approval to operate as a home-based corporation.

Over the years, small corporations have found it advisable to get their charter from the state in which they will be doing the bulk of their business.

Step 2—Name your corporation.

This task would not be difficult if you could give your corporation any name you desired. Such is not the case. You cannot name a corporation without first getting approval from the appropriate authority in the state in which you incorporate.

This approval is necessary for three reasons: The state doesn't want a duplication of names. Nor does it want the public deceived. Finally, it wants to make certain your name tells one and all that they are dealing with a corporation because—as we have seen— owners of corporations usually are not responsible for acts of the corporation.

Let's consider these three reasons in detail:

Obviously, corporations spend much time and money to build a reputation. It would be unfair for someone to come along and capitalize on all that effort by using a similar name. Hence you may not call your motel the Howard-Johnson Motor Lodge. Nor might you open a department store and incorporate it as Sears, Roebuck—or even Spears and Roebuck. And you would find it impossible to start a General Motors Garage Corporation.

The name you choose not only must not duplicate the name of

an existing corporation registered in your state; it cannot even come close. For example, the J.S. Dodge Company was rejected because there already existed in the state a J.S. Dodge Stationery Company. The New Mount Hope Cemetery Association was barred from using that name because there was a Mount Hope Cemetery Association. And the name, American Glucose Sugar Refining Company, was prohibited because there was a Glucose Sugar Refining Company. In Ohio, a hotel firm that wanted to incorporate as the St. Nicholas Plaza, Inc., couldn't do so because another firm, the St. Nicholas Hotel Co., was still in existence.

On the other hand, the United Electric Supply Company was allowed to use that name even though there was a United Electric Fixture and Supply Company in operation. An Ohio court ruled in this case that "there was no evidence of deceptive intent in the use of such name and only inconsequential evidence of confusion."

Most states also forbid the use of certain words which would give the public wrong ideas about the corporation's powers or purposes. Indiana law, for example, stipulates that the corporate name may not imply any purpose or power which is not legally possessed by corporations organizable under the Indiana General Corporation Act. Examples of words or phrases which may not be used are: rural loan and saving association, credit union, banking, railroad, insurance, surety, trust, safe deposit, mortgage, guaranty, or building and loan association. Likewise, such terms as 'police' or 'sheriff' which imply governmental affiliation may not be used.

New York State prohibits in a business corporation title the use of any of the following words or phrases or their abbreviations:

acceptance	doctor	mortgage
annuity	endowment	savings
assurance	fidelity	state police
bank	finance	state trooper
benefit	guaranty	surety
board of trade	indemnity	tenant relocation
bond	insurance	title
casualty	investment	trust
chamber of commerce	lawyer	underwriter
community renewal	loan	urban development
		urban relocation

To alert the public to the fact that they are dealing with a corporation, your title usually must include the word corporation, company, incorporated, or limited—or the appropriate abbreviation of any of those words.

As you think about specific names for your corporation, consider this advice from state officials involved in affirming and rejecting proposed titles. They urge you not to use intials alone. For example, don't call your corporation J.F.K., Inc., or the HMH Corp., because chances of having such a name approved are slim. Your prospects are better if you call your firm the HMH Catering Service or RMP Industrial Designers.

It may also be impossible to get approval for a last name—The Kirk Corporation, say. Even if the name selected is your family name, it is likely to be already in use. Few surnames are not duplicated by the thousands and if yours is a fairly common name the odds are strongly against your being the first to use it for a corporation.

If you feel strongly about using a family name, you can greatly improve your chances by elaborating on it, as in Brown's Plumbing Corporation, the John Brown Appliance Repair Company, or John F. Brown's Garage, Inc. While there might be a John Brown's Bakery Company in your state already, it would not conflict with John F. Brown's Garage.

To further improve your chances of having a family name accepted, add another name to the title. The odds are obviously high against another individual in your state combining two surnames the same as those you have chosen. For instance, the names Huddleston-Brown Metal Works Company, Inc. or Huddleston & Brown Interior Decorators, Inc. are unlikely to be in use already.

Clearly, the more specific you are in the choice of your name, the less chance that it will be rejected by the authorities.

What should you do when you have selected a name that is quite specific, alerts the public to the fact you're a corporation, and does not infringe on another's name?

You will do best to get it cleared by the state authorities as quickly as possible so you don't risk having another incorporator submit a similar name ahead of you.

Do not yield to the temptation to wait until all your incorporating details are wrapped up before submitting a name for approval. A good corporate name that enhances your corporation's image is hard to find. Once you have uncovered such an asset, it would be unbusinesslike to risk losing it.

The best way to protect your selected name is to have it cleared before submitting all the necessary papers. When you learn that the name is available, you can ask that it be reserved for you. Most states will reserve a name for two months and chances are you can get an extension if your incorporating process drags on longer than that.

To determine if your chosen name is available, write to your state's Secretary of State or to the Commissioner of Corporations at your state capital, briefly describing the nature of your corporation's business and listing four or five proposed names in order of preference.

Do not send just one name, because if it is rejected you will have to start again from scratch. The authorities will approve the first available name on the list.

State in your letter that you would like your approved name reserved. Some states charge a small fee for this service. As noted, protecting a good name is well worth the minimal added expense.

In response to your letter, you will receive notification stating which corporate name, if any, has been approved. You also will be told for how long the name will be kept waiting for you. Or you will be asked to submit a reservation form and/or reservation fee.

Step 3—Settle the Questions of Stock.

You must now decide what kinds of stock you will have; how many shares of the total stock you will authorize; how many shares will be issued or sold at the time of incorporation; what value to assign to each share; and whether a stockholder may use property or services in lieu of cash in exchange for stock.

Most small corporations have only one or two kinds of stock:

• Common stock. The ordinary stock of the corporation, it generally entitles the owner to one vote for each share held plus the right to dividends when declared. The common stockholder also has a right to share in the assets of the corporation if and when it is dissolved. If all your investors are more or less on an equal basis, you will probably issue only this class of stock.

• Preferred stock. The preferred stockholder is entitled to a certain specified dividend (you set the amount per share in advance) before dividends are paid to the common shareholders. Typically, holders of the preferred stock do not vote. But some corporate charters provide that if the preferred stockholders do not get their specified dividends over a specified time span, they may legally take over the voting rights or share them with the common stockholders. This is a way to protect preferred holders who otherwise would have no control over management's actions—or inactions.

Preferred stock may be cumulative or non-cumulative. Cumulative preferred stock lets the holder carry over his priority claim when no dividends are declared. He is then entitled to his accumulated back dividends before any dividends may be paid to common stockholders. Unless there is a clear indication to the contrary, preferred stock is always deemed to be cumulative.

Preferred stock may also be participating and non-participating. Participating stock gives the holder the right to share with common stockholders on some stated basis in additional dividend distributions after regular dividends on the preferred stock have been paid. Unless otherwise stated, preferred stock is always considered to be non-participating.

Preferred stock may also be deferred, which means the stock shall be non-cumulative to a certain date and cumulative thereafter. Your corporation could be enabled to get on its feet financially before being obliged to pay any dividends on its preferred stock.

Here are other important factors concerning stock in your new corporation:

• You can transfer assets in an existing firm tax-free. Many business owners fear that incorporating an existing business—a sole proprietorship or partnership—could bring with it some federal or state taxes. While you obviously transfer assets from the going business into the new corporation, federal laws permit such transfers on a tax-free basis if you meet one test.

This test requires that you control at least 80 percent of the new corporation. Thus you must hold a minimum of 80 percent of stock with voting power and at least 80 percent of the total of all non-voting stock.

When you have such control, you can turn your proprietorship or partnership assets over to the corporation without recognizing a gain or loss on the deal. In turn, your corporation doesn't record a gain or a loss when it gives you shares of its stock in exchange for your existing business.

• In many cases, the major tax effect when sole proprietors and partners incorporate is that they must now file two returns—one listing personal income and expenses and the other showing corporate transactions.

There may be complications if you receive cash in the exchange as well as stock. The cash received will be regarded as taxable income. If the new corporation has more liabilities than assets, the excess of liabilities over assets will be regarded as a cash payment to the incorporator.

• The I.R.S. warns that "if your principal purpose in arranging for the assumption of liabilities by the new corporation is to avoid federal income tax on the exchange or, if not for that purpose, there is not a bona fide business purpose, the assumption of liabilities by the corporation will be treated as money received by you."

The vast majority of businesses and professional practices that incorporate are profitable enterprises with more assets than liabilities, however, and the incorporations occur on a tax-free basis.

• Most states require that a firm must have a specified amount of assets before it can be granted a corporate charter. That amount—in cash, accounts receivable, inventories, equipment, etc.—is usually $1,000.

• Incorporation fees are generally based on the amount of stock issued and the par value placed upon each share. If you plan to run a closely-held corporation with yourself and perhaps a few family members as shareholders, you need no more than the number of shares with the lowest par value that qualifies for the lowest state fee. Probably most U.S. firms are incorporated with 200 shares of common stock with no par value.

• The number of shares in your corporation and the par value assigned to them have nothing to do with its total assets. If your firm is worth $500,000 and has only 100 shares, each common share is worth $5,000. If it has 100,000 shares, each share is worth only $5—regardless of the par value printed on the common stock certificate.

• The par value you assign to each share has little significance. If you assign a high par value, your balance sheet will show a high invested capital. If you assign a low or no par value, the balance sheet will show a low figure as invested capital but a higher figure as paid-in surplus. The actual value of each share of your stock in the real world will depend, of course, on whether or not your company prospers.

Placing of a par value has in past years been viewed as a representation that the corporation has received money, goods or services at least equal to the stated value of each share it has issued. State laws, in an attempt to protect investors and creditors alike, have required that par value shares be issued only for money, property, or services of a value at least equal to the par value of the shares issued.

• There is nothing illegal about paying for shares of stock in your corporation with personal services or property—under two conditions.

First, if services are offered in lieu of cash to buy the shares, the services must have been performed and they must be valued at the going rate of such services.

Second, property must be appraised by an independent appraiser. Shares exchanged for the property may not exceed in value that dollar amount set by the appraisal.

• If yours is a small corporation, do not authorize a large number of shares. Since many states charge a filing fee based on the number of shares you have authorized, it is wiser to issue as few shares as possible. Typically, 200 shares will do the trick.

It is also sound business not to issue all of the authorized shares. Keep back one-third to one-half. In that way you will be able to take in additional investors later—or reward an employee—without having to amend the corporation charter to allow you to authorize additional shares.

Step 4—Fill out and file the certificate of incorporation.

You cannot be legally stopped from going into a legitimate business for yourself as a sole proprietor or from forming a partnership with one or more people whenever you feel like it.

Such is not the case when you incorporate a business. To be on safe ground legally, you must have the state's explicit permission to operate. Without it, you violate the law if you represent your enterprise as a corporation.

You obtain this permission by preparing a certificate of incorporation and submitting that form to the appropriate authority in your state for approval.

When the state approves your application, it admits your company into the ranks of corporations with precise purposes and powers.

The certificate you must prepare is a relatively simple form. Since each state's requirements are different—mostly to a small degree—the information required of you varies somewhat. In the main, you will have to provide the following:

• Name of corporation.
• Address of its main office.
• Its purpose.
• Amount of authorized capital stock (total amount of all stock issued), number and type of shares to be issued, and value

and voting rights, if any, of each type of stock.
- Amount of capital stock to be issued at the birth of the corporation.
- Whether the stockholders will buy the stock with cash, by personal services or by transferring property to the corporation.
- Desired lifetime of the corporation—perpetual or for a stated period.
- Names and addresses of the organizing board of directors.
- Name and address of each incorporator plus a statement of the number of shares each incorporator has agreed to buy.

Of these questions, perhaps the most critical relates to your corporation's purpose. In some states you will be cemented into your purpose once you get your charter, unable to expand into other areas without petitioning for an amendment to the charter. For example, a corporation that describes its purpose as the operation of an automobile dealership would not have the power to operate a bakery.

Because states insist that any transaction engaged in by the corporation be reasonably related to its avowed purpose, it makes sense to give your corporation broad powers so that in future years you may move into new areas if you wish to do so.

Your best bet: Aim for an all-purpose charter. Many states do not object to what your corporation proposes to do as long as you do not break federal or state laws. Here is a typical statement lawyers use in applying for an all-purpose charter: "To engage in any lawful act or activity for which corporations may be organized."

Armed with that kind of statement, your corporation could freely buy and sell any and all products and offer any and all services within the law without exceeding its lawful powers. Note, however, that your state may require you to be more explicit. Not all allow all-purpose charters.

As a practical matter, how important is it for a corporation to operate within the powers given to it by the state? It's not ordinarily important—until you find yourself in a courtroom because your corporation is sued for activities it engaged in outside the boundaries of its stated purpose.

Say your corporate charter lets you operate a glove manufacturing business. You have been doing it for three years. Then you become acquainted with two men—specialists in baking French pastries—who wish to start a business in your community.

You persuade them to buy some of your corporation's stock.

You take them on as stockholder-employees and open a pastry shop under your original corporate charter.

Years pass without difficulty. Then a few children who ate some of your shop's tarts wind up ill in the hospital. Their parents start a suit and it is learned that the pastry shop is owned by your glove company. It also becomes known that your corporation is not and has not been permitted to enter the bakery business. Indeed, its corporate charter limits it to the manufacturing of gloves. At that point, you are a very vulnerable businessman—personally vulnerable.

You can see from all of this that where it is permitted, the universal-purpose charter makes far more sense than saying flatly: "To make gloves."

Luckily, errors of judgment that later reveal themselves in your corporate charter need not tie you down forever. You can change details of your charter—and as frequently as you wish. It will cost you time and money to do so, of course, and your changes must conform to state regulations covering any certificate of incorporation.

You may amend your corporation's certificate of incorporation:

- To change its corporate name.
- To enlarge, limit or otherwise change its corporate purposes.
- To specify or change the location of the office of the corporation.
- To specify or change the post office address to which the Secretary of State shall mail a copy of any process against the corporation.
- To make, revoke or change the designation of a registered agent, or to specify or change the address of its registered agent.
- To extend the duration of the corporation or, if the corporation ceased to exist because of the expiration of the duration specified in its certificate of incorporation, to revive its existence.
- To increase or decrease the aggregate number of shares, or shares of any class or series, with or without par value, which the corporation shall have authority to issue.
- To remove from authorized shares any class of shares, or any shares of any class, whether issued or unissued.
- To increase the par value of any authorized shares of any class with par value, whether issued or unissued.
- To reduce the par value of any authorized shares of any class with par value, whether issued or unissued.

● To change any authorized shares, with or without par value, whether issued or unissued, into a different number of shares of the same class or into the same or a different number of shares of any one or more classes or any series thereof, either with or without par value.

● To fix, change, or abolish the designation of any authorized class or any series thereof or any of the relative rights, preferences and limitations of any shares of any authorized class or any series thereof, whether issued or unissued, including any provisions in respect to any undeclared dividends, whether or not cumulative or accrued, or the redemption of any shares, or any sinking fund for the redemption or purchase of any shares, or any preemptive right to acquire shares or other securities.

● To strike out, change or add any provision, not inconsistent with any statute of the state relating to the business of the corporation, its affairs, its rights or powers or the rights or powers of its shareholders, directors or officers.

Major changes will require the approval of the holders of the majority of outstanding voting shares. (That requirement is academic if you are the major stockholder.) Lesser changes—such as moving the office to a different location—may simply need the authorization of your board of directors.

In addition to the stated purposes for which the corporation is organized, it has broad powers to engage in all those actions that may be necessary to help it achieve its objectives. A section of the Model Act, followed in identical or similar form by all states, stipulates that each corporation shall have power:

● To have perpetual succession by its corporate name unless a limited period of duration is stated in its Articles of Incorporation.

● To sue and be sued, complain and defend, in its corporate name.

● To have a corporate seal which may be altered at pleasure, and to use the same by causing it, or a facsimile thereof, to be impressed or affixed or in any other manner reproduced.

● To purchase, take, receive, lease, or otherwise acquire, own, hold, improve, use and otherwise deal in and with, real or personal property, or any interest therein, wherever situated.

● To sell, convey, mortgage, pledge, lease, exchange, transfer and otherwise dispose of all or any part of its property and assets.

● To lend money and use its credit to assist its employees.

● To purchase, take, receive, subscribe for, or otherwise acquire, own, hold, vote, use, employ, sell, mortgage, lend, pledge, or otherwise dispose of, and otherwise use and deal in and with, shares or other interests in, or obligations of, other domestic or foreign corporations, associations, partnerships or individuals, or direct or indirect obligations of the United States or of any other government, state, territory, governmental district or municipality or of any instrumentality thereof.

• To make contracts and guarantees and incur liabilities, borrow money at such rates of interest as the corporation may determine, issue its notes, bonds, and other obligations, and secure any of its obligations by mortgage or pledge of all or any of its property, franchises and income.

• To lend money for its corporate purposes, invest and reinvest its funds, and take and hold real and personal property as security for the payment of funds so loaned or invested.

• To conduct its business, carry on its operations and have offices and exercise the powers granted by this act, within or without the state.

• To elect or appoint officers and agents of the corporation, and define their duties and fix their compensation.

• To make and alter by-laws, not inconsistent with its articles of incorporation or with the laws of the state, for the administration and regulation of the affairs of the corporation.

• To make donations for the public welfare or for charitable, scientific or educational purposes.

• To transact any lawful business which the board of directors shall find will be in aid of governmental policy.

• To pay pensions and establish pension plans, pension trusts, profit sharing plans, stock bonus plans and other incentive plans for any or all of its directors, officers and employees.

• To be a promoter, partner, member, associate, or manager of any partnership, joint venture, trust or other enterprise.

• To have and exercise all powers necessary or convenient to effect its purposes.

Once the certificate of incorporation form has been completed and signed, deliver or mail that document to the proper authorities in your state along with the required filing fee.

Those fees vary from state to state. They are generally based on the total par value of all shares named in the certificate of incorporation. For example, in California, the filing fee as of 1974 was $25 when the aggregate par value of all shares was $75,000 or less; $75 when the aggregate par value was over $75,000 but not over $500,000; and $100 when the aggregate par value was over

$500,000 and not over $1,000,000. When the aggregate par value was over $1,000,000, the filing fee was $100 plus $50 for each $500,000 or fraction of it over the million dollars. If you assigned no par value to your shares, the California law assigned them a value of $10 per share in computing filing fees. The first annual minimum franchise tax of $200 also had to be paid when the Articles of Incorporation were filed with the Secretary of State.

When Articles of Incorporation are not approved and are returned to the applicant, it is for one of the following reasons, says the Secretary of State for Indiana:

• The name of the corporation is confusingly similar to the name of another corporation authorized to do business in the state.

• The corporate name does not include the word corporation, incorporated, or one of the other words or abbreviations required by state law to show that the company is a corporation.

• The purpose clause contains provisions which are not permitted.

• It is not stated whether the corporation is to be perpetual, or the period of time during which it is to continue is not fixed.

• There is no designation of a resident agent for service of process or of a principal office.

• The addresses given for the office and resident agent are not postal addresses within the state.

• Complete postal addresses are not furnished for the initial board of directors and the incorporators.

• All of the incorporators have not signed in duplicate the articles of incorporation. (Photostatic copies of signatures usually will not suffice.)

• Signature of the notary public and notary seal are omitted.

• The amount of the check for the filing fee is incorrect.

Step 5—Write your corporation's by-laws.

Your by-laws provide for the management of your corporation's internal affairs. They are the rules by which you operate on a daily basis.

Any provision of your by-laws becomes invalid when it conflicts with your corporate charter, the U.S. Constitution, or the statutes of the state of incorporation. Moreoever, no by-laws may violate the vested rights of your stockholders.

Unless otherwise stated, the right and power to make by-laws and to change by-laws resides with the common stockholders. However, some states allow directors to make by-laws relating to their own government—provided they do not conflict with the by-laws set down by the stockholders.

Stockholders are presumed to have knowledge of the by-laws of their corporation, whether or not the by-laws were adopted prior to their investment in the corporation.

Since the by-laws form the rules that govern the inner workings of your corporation, you will do well to devote a good deal of time and thought to them. But you need not write the by-laws from scratch. You will find already-prepared by-laws perfectly serviceable. One set of such by-laws is printed in the appendix. You may use it as is, or change any provisions you dislike.

Here are some of the routine matters your corporation's by-laws must settle one way or another:

● Stockholders' meetings. Time; place; order of business; the procedure by which votes will be cast; definition of a quorum; how proxies will be treated; etc.

● Directors. How many; qualifications; terms of office; how removed; fees paid; how vacancies on board are to be filled; special powers; where to meet; how often; time of meeting; order of business; definition of quorum; how committees will be named; etc.

● Officers. Number; titles; duties; qualifications; powers; how to remove; compensation; etc.

● Financial matters. Fiscal year dates; debt limitations; details of the issuance of capital stock; name of transfer agent and registrar and how such services may be terminated; dividend policy; who has authority to sign checks; who may sign contracts; etc.

Normally, the directors you name to your corporation's board will also be your stockholders. But for different reasons owners of corporations also elect outsiders—lawyers, accountants, key employees, local bank officials, etc.

In itself, there is nothing wrong with naming outsiders. Such men and women can greatly help a fledgling corporation. However, human nature being what it is, you will do well not to name too many of them.

While your stockholders technically control the directors, you can get caught in a family squabble that pits other stockholders —some of whom are directors, others who are not—against you. Upshot: You could be outvoted by your own board.

To avoid that sticky situation if you have already promised

directorships to outsiders, provide in your by-laws that the controlling stockholder (you) can remove any or all directors at any time for any reason.

Step 6—Accept your corporate charter from the state.

If the designated official in your state approves the proposed name of your corporation and determines that the certificate of incorporation contains all the required information and has been properly executed, and that nothing in your proposed activities violates state law or public policy, he will issue your corporation's charter.

If he spots a problem in your certificate of incorporation he will return that form to you, asking for qualifying answers to his specific questions.

Many states require that you file a copy of your charter with the local recording office serving your main address—typically the county clerk's office.

Bear in mind that your charter is a binding contract between your corporation and the state. The state may not repeal or alter it unless it has explicitly reserved the right to do so. Nor may you alter (amend) it—even if your stockholders or the directors of your corporation wish to do so—without getting state permission. Getting such permission usually is a routine procedure.

When your corporation has been given official sanction, you should get a corporation kit. If a lawyer is handling the incorporation proceeding for you, he will get it for you. You may also buy one from legal stationers.

This kit contains 30 or so stock certificates, numbered sequentially and printed with your corporate name. Small companies rarely need more than this number. You will also receive a corporate seal-maker and a loose-leaf book to keep stockholder records and minutes of meetings. On average, a kit will cost about $35.

The corporate seal-maker you will receive is a device that embosses a design with your name on it on any document—such as a contract—that you wish to make official-looking.

Incidentally, use of a seal on corporate documents is no longer required in most states. Typically, Nevada law states that "every corporation, by virtue of its existence as such, shall have power to adopt and use a common seal or stamp, and alter the same at pleasure. But use of a seal or stamp by a corporation on any corporate documents is not necessary. The corporation may use a seal or stamp, if it desires, but such use or nonuse shall not in any way affect the legality of the document."

As a rule, a corporation may use or adopt any seal. The corporation laws of North Carolina declare, for instance, that a corporate seal may consist of "anything found upon a paper and which appears to have been put there by due authority or to have been adopted and used by such authority as and for the seal of the corporation."

In one case, a court ruled that the simple word "seal" with a scroll adopted according to resolutions of the stockholders and directors can serve as the official corporate seal.

Step 7—Hold an organizational meeting.

Once you have received your charter, you will have to round up all parties concerned (incorporators, directors, stockholders) and hold an organizational meeting to get the business going.

In a large corporation there will usually be two separate meetings—an organization meeting and later a meeting of shareholders. In small firms, when the organizers of the corporation are its only shareholders and officers, a combined meeting will suffice. The meeting may be conducted by the lawyer who has handled the incorporation procedure. It need not be, of course, if you have incorporated on your own.

State laws vary regarding who does what at that organizational meeting. In some states, the directors are responsible for adopting the by-laws and electing the officers. In others, those powers may be given to the incorporators or shareholders.

In general, subject to local variations, here is what happens:

At the organization meeting, a quorum of incorporators—those whose names appear on the certificate of incorporation—must be present. One of the incorporators calls the meeting to order and the first order of business is to elect a chairman to preside and a secretary to take down the minutes. The secretary may then read a waiver of notice signed by all the incorporators—a statement that they will not invoke the requirement that they be formally notified of the time and place of the meeting.

Typically, the secretary next states that the certificate of incorporation has been approved by the appropriate state authority and that all the required fees have been paid. The certificate, with the official state stamp, becomes part of the minutes and is kept in the official corporate book.

Next, directors are elected to serve until their election is ratified by the shareholders or a more permanent board is elected. It is customary for the incorporators to authorize the board of directors to distribute stock certificates in exchange for goods, services, or cash. (It is not necessary to hand over a separate stock certificate for each share. Rather, each stockholder receives a certificate—one sheet of paper bearing your corporate name across the front and numbered in sequence—on which is typed the shareholder's name and the number of shares he or she owns. You must account for these certificates in your corporate records of stockholder activities.)

Now the chairman reads the proposed by-laws or distributes copies of them to the directors. The provisions in the by-laws could be debated at this point, but they are usually approved by the directors in a formal vote and adopted as the official by-laws of the corporation.

Directors are also asked to vote on the location of the principal office of the corporation and to authorize the opening of checking and savings accounts in the corporation's name, specifying who is to have the authority to sign checks and make withdrawals.

The first meeting of shareholders is called to order by the chairman elected at the previous meeting. The previously-chosen secretary records the minutes. After it has been established that a quorum of shareholders representing a majority of the outstanding shares are present, and that all shareholders have been notified of the meeting in due time (or have signed waivers of notice), the shareholders usually will be asked to elect a board of directors, president, secretary, treasurer and perhaps other officers. Usually, a motion will be made, seconded and carried that the election of directors and officers at the organization meeting be ratified by the shareholders.

The by-laws will also be presented to the shareholders for their ratification. This too is usually a matter of form. The shareholders will usually also be asked to approve other decisions made at the organization meeting.

The way that meetings of incorporators and shareholders of small corporations are conducted often is less important, legally, than the way the minutes are kept. The latter should show that the shareholders have approved the actions taken by the incorporators and directors so that there can be no kickback from dissident shareholders claiming that their rights were ignored or that they had no chance to debate provisions in the by-laws which they later see as being against their interests.

If you and close family members are the only incorporators and shareholders, you need not be unduly concerned about procedures followed at these meetings. However, your minutes should be in good order. Step by step guidance in the conduct of the organization meeting and shareholders' meetings as well as simplified minutes for your use are provided in the appendix.

When your corporation becomes a legal entity depends on your state of incorporation. In most states a corporation comes into legal existence as soon as the charter has been issued. But other states do not consider the corporation as having an existence of its own until the organizational meeting has been held. Your state may also hold off giving your corporation the green light until a report of your organizational meeting has been mailed to the proper authorities.

OPERATING AS A FOREIGN CORPORATION

Your corporation is a domestic corporation in the state in which it was incorporated. It is a foreign corporation in all the other states. You will have to register in those states as well if you wish to "transact business" within their borders. But you can carry on many activities outside your home state without having to register. Michigan, which is typical of most states in the way it regards corporations formed elsewhere, says "a foreign corporation is *not* considered to be transacting business in this state, for the purposes of this act, solely because it is carrying on in this state any one or more of the following activities:

"Maintaining or defending an action or suit or an administrative or arbitrative proceeding, or effecting the settlement thereof or the settlement of a claim or dispute.

"Holding meetings of its directors or shareholders or carrying on any other activities concerning its internal affairs.

"Maintaining a bank account.

"Maintaining an office or agency for the transfer, exchange, and registration of its securities, or appointing and maintaining a trustee or depository with relation to its securities.

"Effecting sales through an independent contractor.

"Soliciting or procuring orders, whether by mail or through employees or agents or otherwise, where such orders require acceptance without this state before becoming binding contracts.

"Borrowing money, with or without security.

"Securing or collecting debts or enforcing any right in property securing the same.

"Transacting any business in interstate commerce.

"Conducting an isolated transaction not in the course of a number of repeated transactions of like nature."

So much for activities that do not demand that you sign up as a foreign corporation. What are the actions that will require you to file for admittance to a foreign state?

If you set up an office or factory there and hire employees to carry on regular business activities, you must get that state's permission. For instance, a retailer incorporated in New York who later establishes a branch in New Jersey would be required to apply in New Jersey for recognition as a foreign corporation.

Before you register as a foreign corporation, consider these points:

• You may not transact any business which that state's domestic companies are not permitted to transact.

• You will not be admitted to another state if the name of your corporation is the same as or deceptively similar to the name of a domestic corporation in that state.

• You will not be admitted if your corporate name contains any word or phrase that indicates or implies that it will conduct a banking, insurance, or savings business.

• You will not be admitted if your name does not have a word or abbreviation showing it is a corporation.

To get permission to operate as a foreign corporation, you must apply for a certificate of authority. The application you must file generally must contain the same kind of information required in your original certificate in your home state: date of incorporation; period of your corporation's duration; address of its principal office in the state under the laws of which it is organized; names of other states in which the corporation is admitted to conduct business; purpose of the corporation; names and addresses of officers and directors; a statement of capital showing the aggregate number of shares outstanding and their cost; an estimate of the value of property located in the foreign state; an estimate of the gross amount of business expected to be transacted per year in the foreign state.

You must also maintain a registered office and agent once you have received a certificate of authority from the foreign state. The registered office may be the same as the place in which you will be conducting business, but that need not be the case. Your agent must have the same business office as the registered office. The purpose of the registered office and agent is to receive all official notices from the state and to be the one to whom any service or process in any suit may be made.

Your foreign corporation will also have to abide by most of the regulations covering domestic corporations: Pay the necessary fees, both when you apply and when you receive permission to operate. Pay annual state taxes. File an annual report. And you must keep books and records on file at your registered office for stockholder inspection.

What are the penalties for operating in a foreign state without the required authority? A common effect is to prohibit the corporation from further action in the state until it gets its corporate status approved. It must pay all fees, penalties, and franchise taxes which it would have had to pay had it legally applied for and received a certificate of authority for all of the time during which it operated without authority.

On top of that, a requirement in many states calls for a $25 fine for each day the corporation has failed to pay fees, penalties, and franchise taxes.

The fact that a corporation entered a foreign state and did business there without permission does not invalidate any contracts that corporation made. The illegal corporation may be sued in the foreign state but in some cases it may not sue.

HOW TO DEDUCT YOUR INCORPORATING COSTS

Now that you have incorporated successfully and are operational, you will do well to total up the costs incurred in incorporating. Such expenses are, for the most part, tax-deductible. The rules on how you handle this deduction differ, however, from those surrounding typical business expenses.

You may deduct virtually all your costs of incorporation proportionately over any period of time you choose that is longer than 60 months. Your starting date is the first month in which your corporation is considered in business.

To be deducted in this way, the incorporating expenses must have been incurred before the end of your corporation's first tax year.

Here is what may be deducted: All fees paid to the state relating to the incorporation; necessary accounting fees; legal fees for the preparation of the corporate charter, by-laws, etc.; costs of holding organizational meetings; expenses of temporary directors who served before the permanent board was elected.

Certain items are not deductible. They include expenses connected with the sale of corporate stock, which is regarded as a reduction of the non-taxable proceeds from the sale of stock, and costs related to the transfer of assets to the corporation.

You must report to the I.R.S. how you intend to take those cost-of-incorporating deductions. Your report is appended to your corporation's tax return for the first tax year it is actively in business. The report should describe the amount and nature of your expenditures, and point out the number of months (60 or more) over which you intend to deduct them. Adherence to the self-imposed timetable is mandatory.

What if you do not take this long-term tax deduction? You may consider your expenses as capital expenditures and add them to the cost of the corporation. When you sell or dissolve the corporation, your incorporation costs will be included in your cost basis and thereby lower your taxable profit.

4.
Regulations You Must Observe
In Operating Your Corporation

The state in which you incorporate is concerned about stockholders who may invest money in your operation. Naturally, it does not want to see them fleeced. It is especially interested in the plight of minority stockholders—individuals unrelated to the majority stockholder or stockholders in control of your corporation. They must be protected as fully as possible because they have no real say in running the corporation.

Of particular concern to the state is the ability of persons who own most of a corporation's shares to singlehandedly decide its course of action. Such power is legal. But it must not be exercised in a way that injures other stockholders.

As a consequence, you are expected to follow certain state regulations as you conduct your corporate business. These regulations cover such things as the election of a board of directors; the duties and responsibilities not only of the board but also of the president, secretary, and treasurer; how annual meetings are to be held and how directors are to be elected; how shareholders are to be notified of meetings to be held and of the reasons for holding them; and so on.

How do such regulations affect you and your corporation? The answer realistically depends on the number of your stockholders and their relationship to you.

Understand that the state's emphasis is on stockholder protection. So if your corporation has stockholders unrelated to you or the other officers of your firm, you'll do well to follow the rules to the letter.

But if you have a small operation and do not intend to broaden your stockholder base beyond yourself, your spouse and your children, you can conceivably violate the rules and keep out of trouble with the state authorities.

As a rule, the I.R.S. is concerned only with your taxes. An agent auditing your books will pay scant attention to violations of state regulations regarding annual meetings, minutes of meetings and elections of directors that he may come across. He will want to see that you "act as a corporation" only where tax matters are involved.

Why such laxity? For one reason, because the respective states lack the time or inclination to supervise closely the activities of the many thousands of small corporations within their borders. As a result, many small corporations ignore not only state laws but their own by-laws as well.

For example, a contractor who has owned a small corporation in New York for 13 years has never held an annual meeting and has kept no minutes of directors' meetings because no such meetings ever took place. He has no idea of the whereabouts of his third director, a man elected for a three-year term when the corporation was formed who has not been seen since. No state authority has ever checked his records for corporate compliance.

It appears that the state concerns itself with corporate behavior only when someone—typically, a disgruntled stockholder—screams about irregularities and management's high-handed tactics which have cost him some or all of his investment. If you have no other stockholders, obviously no one will "blow the whistle."

While it is sometimes possible to violate the rules with abandon, this information is in the same category as the comment of a motorist-friend who says that he regularly exceeds highway speed limits by 20 m.p.h. without being stopped. You just might be the one to get caught.

There are practical reasons for obeying the law. For example:

If your corporation should go bankrupt, your creditors in a routine legal maneuver may subpoena your records. If they find that you have not been running a true corporation, you may not have the ability to walk safely away from your company's debts. Those hungry creditors may be able to sue you personally for the money owed them. Your personal assets—your home, say—can be tapped.

The second example is not as severe, but perhaps more likely. It is coercion. If you don't want to risk being backed into a corner by a stockholder who "knows his rights," follow the corporate rules exactly. To do otherwise is to invite corporate "blackmail."

Third, benefits you hand out to yourself and your officers but neglect to give your employees may be denied a tax deduction by an I.R.S. agent auditing your firm unless your board has approved such additional bonuses and approval has been recorded in the minutes of a board meeting. "No minutes, no additional benefits," observes one tax specialist.

Some corporations today approve at a board meeting and then place in the minutes the resolution that if the I.R.S. rules officers' salaries too high, the affected officers will return the overage to the corporation. While the corporation is taxed on its additional income, the officers may treat the extra funds as a loan they have had for a year or more, provided they pay back interest on the loan. If that policy were not clearly stated in the minutes of the board meeting, the officers would be forced to treat the extra funds as dividend income, taxable at their highest personal rates.

Running your corporation with the required meetings, elections, and record-keeping is sound business practice.

THE ROLES OF DIRECTORS, OFFICERS, SHAREHOLDERS

The rules under which your firm must operate to qualify as a bona fide corporation are set down in the corporate laws of your state. They are fairly consistent, differing in different states only in minor ways.

In some instances, you will have no choice but to comply. On other matters, you may choose different provisions and operating regulations.

However, you will find it most convenient and less complicated if you operate your corporation within the standard framework and take as few permissible exceptions as possible.

Duties of Directors

Your corporation must be managed by a board of directors—each of whom usually must be over 21 years of age. Ordinarily, you'll need at least three directors. When all the shares are owned by fewer than three people, the number of directors required may be fewer than three—but not fewer than the number of shareholders you have. Most small corporations in the United States have a board consisting of two directors—the owner-husband and his wife.

Whether you have two directors or 18, those directors have broad powers. Typically, they make all significant corporate decisions unless your state sets some limitations.

However, you may limit their powers by inserting specific restrictions in your by-laws. For example, you may reserve to the stockholders the right to approve or disapprove the borrowing of money beyond a certain maximum, or the hiring of executives to fill certain positions within the corporation, particularly the presidential post since it is a key one. (Such provisions protect shareholders who do not take an active part in the firm's management by guaranteeing that important decisions which might affect the value of their holdings will not be taken without their consent.)

As a rule, directors retain the right to hire officers of the corporation, determine corporate policy, authorize loans, approve or disapprove the pension plan, authorize the purchase of real estate, and so on.

Since the directors hold such power, they may often be held personally responsible for the good management of the corporation. They are expected to make certain that not only the management team but also all other directors live up to their responsibilities to shareholders. When they fail to exercise such supervision, they may make themselves vulnerable to a stockholder suit.

As a general principle, directors are required to exercise diligence, honesty, and reasonable judgment. But the law doesn't demand the impossible. Directors are not held responsible for mistakes they make in good faith as prudent persons. Courts have consistently refused to interfere in the management of a corporation whose directors acted within their powers despite dissenting stockholders' objections.

The states also protect directors when their actions are based on corporate records. Nobody expects a director who, in discharging his duties, believes in and acts on a report a corporate officer or employee gives him only to learn later that the report was inaccurate or fraudulently prepared. Any poor decision made under those circumstances would not be deemed to be the director's fault. Directors need not be clairvoyant.

In more formal language, state laws typically declare that "a director may not be held responsible if, in discharging his duties, he relies on the books and records of the corporation, upon reports made to the corporation by an officer or employee or agent selected with reasonable care, and upon financial statements or written reports prepared by an officer or employee in charge of its accounts, or verified by a public accountant or a firm of public accountants."

. Many states limit a director's term of office to three years. Your by-laws may set different limits within the confines of the state's laws. For example, while your state may say no director's term may run longer than three years, your by-laws may require two-year or even one-year terms. Your by-laws, however, could not set the term at four years.

No state regulation says a director may not run for re-election. So, unless your by-laws say otherwise, a director might be elected from year to year and remain on your board for dozens of years.

At times, of course, a director may not fill out his term. Perhaps he has died, retired from business, or moved to another locale. Or perhaps you have removed him for misconduct or other reasons.

Unless your by-laws provide that the directors shall fill a vacancy on the board, such vacancies may be filled only by shareholder approval. Moreover, a director chosen to fill a vacancy usually holds his position only until the next annual meeting of shareholders, when he may be re-elected or a new director elected.

. The vacancies just discussed are "natural" vacancies that happen in all kinds of corporations. There is another type of vacancy—the "grand slam."

Unless your by-laws prohibit it, those representing a majority of your company's stock—that could be just you—may remove any or all directors without cause. With such power, one stockholder holding more than 50 percent of the shares may run the company as he sees fit, firing any director who disagrees with his policies or displeases him in any way.

Much can be said for this dictatorial approach. It often accomplishes much in minutes. But in large companies particularly, there is a major drawback to the ability to fire all who disagree: Your board will pull in its horns and you'll be surrounded by persons who will agree with every decision you make, even if your judgment causes the corporation to go bankrupt.

Most giant publicly-held corporations have long seen the foolishness of the iron-fish approach. They frequently have a clause in their by-laws stipulating that a director may be removed only for cause by a majority of the entire board.

"Cause" generally means: conviction of a felony; being declared of unsound mind by a court; judged bankrupt; or found engaging in other conduct that causes scandal or is prejudicial to the corporation's best interests.

The board will meet in accordance with rules spelled out in your by-laws. Generally speaking, special meetings may be called either by the board chairman or the president plus two directors.

Notification of a directors' meeting isn't as critical as it is when you must call for a stockholders' meeting. Five days advance notice is considered sufficient notice. Your by-laws—written with your own wishes in mind—will spell out the details surrounding regular and special meetings of the board.

Board decisions are made by a majority of the directors attending the meeting, if there is a formal meeting. But it isn't necessary for the board to hold formal meetings if the by-laws permit another approach. A better way often is to telephone the directors for their advice and votes on some important matter. But a "majority" vote then changes its complexion. It must be a majority of all members of the board. You can't forget to call one or two.

If you have polled your directors by phone on a relatively important issue—say the adoption of plans to expand your present plant—get the directors to sign a written consent to the action they authorized on the phone. Those consents should then be filed with the minutes of the directors' meetings.

Since voting is by majority, it is unwise to appoint an even number of directors who could easily be split down the middle on an issue.

(In rare cases where a board was stymied because there was no tie-breaking vote, courts have appointed a provisional director—considered to have all the rights and powers of the other directors—to vote with one of the two factions after having heard the details surrounding the problem. This outsider must be paid for the time he spends as a provisional director. If there is a dispute surrounding his fee, the court that appointed him will decide on his compensation.)

Minutes of meetings held by your board of directors are important to the smooth functioning of your enterprise. If nothing else, such minutes will from time to time resolve misunderstandings about who said what to whom and why.

But beyond being oil in your corporate machinery, the minutes act as a document of record for outsiders doing business with your corporation.

For instance, before you may open a checking account, you will have to provide the bank with a resolution stating that such is the wish of your board of directors. That resolution is based on the minutes of the meeting at which the directors voted for opening a checking account at such and such a bank. Bankers have their own forms which your corporate secretary may fill out and return.

When you seek a bank loan for your corporation, the bank will want a formal copy of the board's resolution to seek financing. Only the minutes of the board can provide the basis for that resolution. In effect, they prove that the board has authorized such borrowing.

From a record-keeping viewpoint, the minutes are best kept together in what is called the minute book, thereby forming an important history over the years of your corporate activities.

Mostly, the minutes should record actions agreed upon by the board; salaries for the officers; authorization to enter into contracts; an agreement to buy or sell real estate; approval to move the home office to another location.

The board's stands against actions are also important items to be recorded in the minutes. Examples of such refusals: Voted down salary increase for officers; refused to enter into a contract with the ABC Corporation; resolved not to sell the plant in Hackensack; refused to move the home office to Burbank; and so on.

Typically, the corporation secretary keeps the minutes. Frequently, such men or women simply take notes during the meeting, then later type or dictate a "fleshed out" version of the notes that then become the minutes of the meeting.

No special format is required by law. Each corporate secretary is on his own, free to add his style to an important corporate document.

A final note from experienced minute-takers: Don't note most of the words spoken. The results are not worth the effort. Instead simply note the end results of each discussion of a particular topic—omitting the pros and cons surrounding the discussion.

That way you won't waste your time keeping up with the dialogue Kelly and Brown had on why the corporation should and should not move to larger quarters, including Brown's attack on Kelly for changing his mind on this matter.

Later, your minutes will report: Motion to move to larger quarters was rejected, 4 to 2.

Officers You Must Have

Most states require a corporation to have officers with specific titles and responsibilities. You must have a president, a treasurer, and a corporate secretary—not the dictation-taking kind. Some states prohibit the president and the secretary from holding an additional office. Other states allow one person to wear all three hats.

These are the responsibilities of the various officer positions:

● **President:** More times that not, this individual runs the corporation as its chief executive officer. Persons and firms dealing with your corporation are entitled to assume that the president has the authority to make all contracts on its behalf. Thus, a business contract signed by the president usually is regarded by the courts as binding on the corporation. The president also has the authority to institute or defend legal proceedings whenever the directors or shareholders are deadlocked.

● **Corporate Secretary:** This officer has several duties designed to satisfy the record-keeping and reporting requirements of the state. He or she has the responsibility for keeping records of all shareholders' meetings, including records of all votes and minutes of the meetings. The state requires that he or she keep this record in a book at corporate headquarters under his or her control, where it can be made accessible to anyone authorized to examine it. Ordinarily the secretary acts as a voting inspector at stockholder meetings. As such he or she has the duty of keeping on file an up-to-date list of shareholders, preparing a list of those entitled to vote at regular or special meetings, and certifying all votes, resolutions, and actions of the shareholders and the board.

The corporate secretary has no power to bind the corporation by virtue of the office. However, there is a presumption that documents the secretary has marked with the corporate seal are duly authorized documents.

● **Treasurer:** This executive is normally responsible for receiving, disbursing, and maintaining custody of corporate funds. The treasurer does not have the power on his own to borrow money or issue negotiable instruments.

● **Vice Presidents:** These executives have no authority unless they are given some specific function by their superiors. They then have the power to transact the business necessary to carry out that specific function.

● **Stockholders:** They are the owners of a corporation. They choose the directors who thereupon run the business.

Stockholders in small corporations are usually also the officers and directors who operate it. Their role generally differs from that of the typical shareholders of a medium-sized or large corporation, who seldom if ever participate directly in its management. Usually the main interest of outside shareholders is in receiving some of the profits via dividends or capital gains. They may know little about the directors and officers of the corporation.

A shareholder in the larger corporations has little real power, especially when he or she is only one of hundreds or even thousands. The few functions that fall to him are exercised by casting votes at annual and special meetings.

Prior notice must be given the shareholders of record for any meeting they are expected to attend. (A shareholder of record is one listed on the corporation's books as of a certain cut-off date—perhaps a week, ten days, or a month before the meeting notice is mailed.)

Dealing with Your Shareholders

Whether your shareholders are your mother and father, your wife and your brother-in-law, or strangers living all over the U.S.A., you should follow the rules regarding stockholder rights and avoid any possible litigation.

(Squabbles among all-in-the-family stockholders often lead to the alienation of relatives, animosity, hatreds, indeed even family feuds minus only the shooting. There is often more safety in having virtual strangers as stockholders than in having your brother-in-law own 36 percent of your corporation's shares.)

Here is what you should know about your responsibilities to your shareholders.

• **Shareholders' Annual Meeting.** Your by-laws should state when the annual meeting of stockholders for the election of directors will be held. If you overlook that detail when writing your corporate by-laws, you may have to follow the rules of your state. For instance, in Ohio any corporation that has not selected a standard annual meeting date must hold its meeting on "the first Monday of the fourth month following the close of each fiscal year of the corporation."

Many states say, however, that failure to hold the annual meeting at the designated time will not cause a dissolution of the corporation.

As for selecting a site for the annual meeting, most states are just as flexible. Illinois law says, for example, that "meetings of shareholders may be held at such place, either within or without the state, as the by-laws may specify. In the absence of any such provision, all meetings shall be held at the registered office of the corporation of this state."

● **Shareholders' Annual Report.** You will be expected to send your shareholders, prior to your annual meeting, your corporate annual report: a financial statement consisting of a balance sheet and a summary of profit, loss and surplus.

Most states paint a clear picture of what belongs in the balance sheet. For instance, the Ohio corporation law requires:

"A balance sheet containing a summary of the assets, liabilities, stated capital, and surplus (showing separately any capital surplus arising from unrealized appreciation of assets, other capital surplus, and earned surplus) as of a date not more than four months before such meeting;

"A statement of profit and loss and surplus, including a summary of profits, dividends paid, and other changes in the surplus accounts for the period commencing with the date marking the end of the period for which the last preceding statement of profit and loss required under this section was made and ending with the date of said balance sheet, or in the case of the first statement of profit and loss, from the incorporation of the corporation to the date of said balance."

Many states also require that the financial statement contain an opinion signed by the president, vice president, treasurer or assistant treasurer of the corporation or by a public accountant or firm of public accountants to the effect that the statement "presents fairly the financial position of the corporation and the results of its operations in conformity with generally accepted accounting principles applied on a basis consistent with that of the preceding period, or such other opinion as is in accordance with sound accounting practice."

These regulations apply, of course, when there are outside shareholders. The owner of a corporation with only family members as shareholders normally need not be concerned about them.

● **Shareholders' Special Meetings.** A special meeting of stockholders may be called in most states by the president, the board of directors, or other corporate officers if the by-laws give them that authority.

Shareholders have the right in some instances to call a special meeting. Often all it takes is for those owning ten percent or more of all shares entitled to vote, to request in writing that such a meeting be held. Management must comply unless the reason for the meeting is blatantly trivial.

So that corporate life does not become unbearable, however, many managements protect themselves by inserting a statement like this in the by-laws: "Requests by shareholders for special meetings must state the purpose or purposes of the meeting, and the business transacted at that special meeting shall be confined to the stated purpose or purposes."

● **Shareholders' "No-Meeting" Meetings.** If you own a small corporation with all your stockholders in the family, you may find it a nuisance to call them together for this or that meeting—especially if they are not within easy commuting distance.

The law recognizes such problems and allows shareholders to act by written consent rather than by attending a formal meeting and casting their votes in person.

There is a major proviso: In order for your stockholders to meet by mail, you must have the permission of *all* stockholders entitled to vote. One dissenting stockholder can kill the whole deal, force an actual physical meeting to be held, and perhaps set up warring factions that will not be easily reconciled.

● **Shareholders' Notification.** Typical of the laws regarding how stockholders must be notified of an upcoming shareholders' meeting are New York's regulations. They state: "Whenever shareholders are required or permitted to take any action at a meeting, written notice shall be given stating the place, date, and hour of the meeting and—unless the meeting is an annual meeting—indicating that it is being issued by or at the direction of the person or persons calling the meeting."

The notice must also explain the purpose or purposes for which the special meeting has been called.

Most states require that a mailed notice be sent by first class mail not less than ten days nor more than 60 days before the date of the meeting. The notice is considered to be delivered to the shareholder when it is dropped into the mail box and addressed to him or her at the address appearing on the membership books of the corporation.

If the notice is hand-delivered, it must be given to the shareholder not less than five nor more than 60 days before the meeting date.

Once the mailing has been made or the notices hand-delivered, the officer of your corporation in charge of the mailing should sign a statement that it was made in compliance with the law. Such a statement is generally accepted in a court if a question of stockholders' rights arises later.

Your by-laws may or may not require that you give another notice to your shareholders if an originally scheduled meeting started as planned but was adjourned for any reason. If your by-laws overlook this contingency, you will have to abide by the law of your state. Most times, it says if the new time and place to which the meeting is adjourned are announced at the original session—and no additional business will be transacted at the new meeting other than the subjects originally announced for the first meeting—there is no need to notify shareholders of the new time and place. Usually, however, shareholders must be notified if a new date and place are set for the adjourned meeting after the adjournment.

● **Shareholders' Quorum.** Either the certificate of incorporation or your by-laws will state how many stockholders will be regarded as constituting a quorum for a meeting. Holders of a majority of the voting shares ordinarily constitute a quorum. You are free to set your own rules in this regard, however.

An interesting and sometimes perplexing question often arises when quorums are discussed. Say a meeting begins with the legally required number of shareholders present. During the meeting, several stockholders leave so that a quorum is no longer present. May the remaining shareholders continue to conduct business legally?

Answer: Yes. When a quorum is once present to organize a meeting, it is not later broken if and when attending shareholders walk out and do not return.

● **Counting Shareholder Votes.** When directors are to be elected, most states permit election by a "plurality of the votes cast at a meeting by the stockholders entitled to vote in the election."

What that means is this: If three directors are to be elected, the three candidates with the greatest number of votes are the winners. Each of those candidates need not have received 51 percent of the votes. If a large number of persons have been nominated, directors could be elected with only a small percentage of the total vote cast.

A few corporations permit an optional method for voting: The cumulative plan.

Under this plan, a shareholder may cumulate his votes by giving one candidate a number of votes equal to the number of directors to be elected, multiplied by the number of shares he owns. Say three directors are to be elected. The shareholder owning 200 shares might cast 600 votes (3 directors times 200 shares) for one director.

Some corporations allow the shareholder to spread his cumulative votes among more than one director—400, say, for John Jones, and 200 for Henry Smith.

Cumulative voting gives minority shareholders a chance to be represented on the board of directors by allowing them to heavily support the candidate they believe will best protect their interests.

For the most part, however, corporations abide by the statutory voting plan. That method allows one vote for each share of stock held. This method of counting votes permits the biggest shareholders to control the corporation with little or no interference.

What about other corporate activities that stockholders must approve?

When any corporate activity other than the election of directors requires approval, state laws customarily require that such action be authorized by a majority of the total votes cast by stockholders attending the meeting and by those who have sent in proxies.

A proxy is a legal form that enables a stockholder to vote at a meeting without attending it. In most states, a shareholder entitled to vote may authorize another person to act for him or her by proxy. Managements of large corporations simplify the situation by mailing out a proxy form along with a notice of the meeting so that shareholders need not scratch around for a form on their own. A sample of a proxy form for the election of directors will be found in the appendix.

Using the proxy method, a shareholder can delegate either to management or to a group opposing management the right to vote his shares in his absence.

● **Shareholders' Rights.** Apart from the right to vote in accordance with the by-laws, shareholders generally have two other rights, one of which they are slowly losing. They have the right to see books and records of the corporation—with certain qualifications. They also have the right not to have their holdings watered down by the offering of additional shares of stock—the right that is eroding.

A shareholder attending a shareholders' meeting may legally ask (and such a request must be fulfilled) for an alphabetically arranged list—kept in orderly fashion—of the stockholders of record who are entitled to vote, showing their respective addresses and the number and class of shares held by each one. You or another officer of your corporation must certify that the list is accurate.

Every stockholder also has the right to examine, in person or through an agent or attorney, the articles of your corporation, its regulations, books and records of account, minutes and records of shareholders, and voting trust agreements. Such an authorized visitor must also be permitted to make copies or extracts of such documents. There usually are two provisos set down by law: The visit must be made at a reasonable time—typically, during the 9 to 5 business day; and the examination must have a reasonable and proper purpose.

Do not think it is easy to keep your records secret by replying that the stockholder's visit is unreasonable or is for an unworthy purpose. Several court cases have established that the burden of proving that the stockholder lacks a valid reason for inspecting corporate records rests on your shoulders. The courts have ruled that if the shareholder's request is in writing, you are expected to honor it "within a reasonable time."

Some states require that an individual seeking to examine corporate records must have been a shareholder for at least six months or must own at least five percent of all outstanding shares.

A common provision of state corporation laws stipulates that an officer or agent of a corporation who refuses to let a shareholder, his agent or lawyer examine the books and records for proper purposes will have to pay the shareholder. The corporation also will be subject to a fine imposed by the state, usually $50 or so.

These are the details about the rights which allow stockholders to keep their relative share in the corporation by buying a proportionate amount of any new stock offering that their corporation makes:

Say a shareholder owns 20 percent of the total outstanding shares of a corporation that intends to increase its capital by offering more shares for sale. He or she must be allowed to buy (*before* non-stockholders) enough shares to keep his or her holdings at the 20 percent level.

This provision is often included in the Articles of Incorporation of small corporations to insure that the rights of all shareholders will be protected by making it impossible to dilute their holdings through the offering of shares to outsiders.

For example, four brothers together own 53 percent of a small manufacturing company's shares. They do not participate in the day-to-day management. However, they share the same outlook on the company, its products and its future, and as a result they usually vote in unison. Thanks to "preemptive rights," they will retain that 53 percent control as long as they choose—despite any future offering of shares to others. Any time a new stock offering is made, they have the right to buy sufficient shares to keep their combined ownership at its present level.

Many larger corporations are dropping the provision for preemptive rights from their Articles of Incorporation, however. Over a 10-year period, 200 companies listed on The New York Stock Exchange amended their charters to abolish it.

• **Maintenance of Records.** The state in which you incorporate will insist that your corporation keep accurate records of books of account, together with minutes of the incorporators' proceedings, shareholders and directors' meetings, and committee meetings held by several of the directors. You must also maintain a list of your stockholders, showing their addresses and the number and class of shares issued or transferred to them. Your stockholder list must be kept up to date.

Although the record-keeping rules are applied strictly in the cases of large corporations with hundreds of stockholders, they apply equally to smaller, non-public firms with few shareholders—the closely-held corporation.

In fact, it is often in small firms where a handful of persons own all the stock that dissident shareholders insist that the laws concerning corporate books and records be followed most strictly.

Even if all the other stockholders in your closely-held corporation now seem to be friendly, you will do well to abide by the rules. Bear in mind that a friendly stockholder today may become an outraged one tomorrow. A stockholder wife or husband may be a friend indeed; but a stockholder ex-wife or ex-husband may be determined to make life miserable for you.

WHEN YOU MAY AND MAY NOT PAY DIVIDENDS

To protect creditors, and in some cases minority stockholders, state laws regulate the conditions under which your corporation may and may not pay cash dividends. Usually a corporation may declare and pay dividends—once the board of directors has so voted—subject to the following provisions:

● You may not pay a dividend when the corporation is insolvent, when its net assets are less than its stated capital, or when payment of the dividends would make the corporation insolvent or reduce its net assets below its stated capital.

● You may pay a dividend out of paid-in surplus or surplus arising from the surrender to the corporation of any of its shares that have a preferential right to receive dividends. But you must tell your shareholders the source of those dividends when you mail out their checks.

● You may not pay a dividend out of a surplus that arises from the unrealized appreciation in value of—or the re-valuation of—corporate assets. Suppose a building your corporation owns suddenly increases sharply in its market value thanks to neighborhood developments. Can you distribute that increase in the property's value as dividends? No. The fact that your corporation is now worth more on paper would not justify declaring dividends. If you sold the property—and actually realized the profit—you could be in a dividend-paying position.

● You may not pay a dividend on treasury shares—unless you pay an equivalent dividend on all corporate shares outstanding at the same time.

What about stock dividends? There are few restrictions on them. When you give shareholders additional shares in the corporation, you do not increase each shareholder's equity. The increased number of shares is divided into the same assets, so stock dividends simply decrease proportionately the amount of assets standing behind each share. Remember, however, that no stock dividend can be paid in shares that are given a preference as to dividends over the shares upon which no dividend is paid—unless that kind of stock dividend has been authorized by the articles of incorporation.

RULES COVERING MERGER OR CONSOLIDATION

State laws also specify the procedure you must follow when your corporation seeks to merge or consolidate with another business or to consolidate two or more affiliated corporations into a new corporation.

The board of directors of each corporation contemplating

merger or consolidation must approve a resolution that contains the precise plan of merger or consolidation.

This plan must:

● Name the corporations proposing to merge and also name the corporation into which they propose to merge—usually known as the surviving corporation.

● Set down terms and conditions of the proposed merger and how they will be put into effect.

● Explain the manner of converting shares of each of the merging corporations into shares, obligations or other securities of the surviving corporation.

● Include a statement of the changes in the Articles of Incorporation that the surviving corporation must enact to reconcile conflicting interests of the merging corporations.

Most states require corporate directors who have approved a plan of merger or consolidation to submit the plan to shareholders at the annual meeting or at a meeting called especially to vote on it.

A written or printed notice of the meeting must be delivered by hand or by mail to each shareholder of record entitled to vote. The notice must be sent at least 15 to 20 days before the meeting date. It usually must be accompanied by a detailed statement summarizing the plan of merger or consolidation, including up-to-date balance sheets and income statements from each corporation involved.

It is also customary for the states to require that two-thirds of the outstanding shares of each of the corporations involved approve the plan of merger or consolidation. Exceptions to the rule requiring two-thirds approval are found in "liberal" states like Delaware and Nevada. There you will need only a simple majority—more than 50 percent—of stockholders' approving votes to make the merger legal.

Another exception, found in many states, exists when one corporation owns at least 90 percent of the outstanding shares of each class of stock of the second corporation. Then no stockholder approval is required. Generally needed in such cases is only the directors' approval, along with the filing of a statement to that effect with authorities of the state of incorporation. In such cases, the parent corporation is considered the surviving corporation.

Rights of Disapproving Stockholders

A stockholder who opposes a plan to merge or consolidate usually has the right to pull out of the corporation, selling his shares at "fair value." This provision of the law typically comes into play when stock in a closely-held corporation is inherited by many different persons, often family members with different ideas about the direction the firm should take.

A shareholder who disapproves of a plan to merge or consolidate can file objections in writing before or at the shareholders' meeting at which the plan is submitted to a vote.

If the unhappy stockholder votes against the plan, he or she may demand, within 20 days after the merger or consolidation takes effect, that the surviving corporation pay a fair price for the shares. The value must be determined as of the day prior to the stockholders' meeting.

Disputes over fair value of shares in closely-held corporation are common, because there is often a sharp difference between the asset value per share and what each share might bring if offered for sale to the public. Often a market price will be much higher or lower than the dollar value of plant, equipment, inventories, etc., that stands behind each share.

Usually a provision in state law spells out how fair value is to be determined. The shareholder and the surviving corporation generally are given a month to settle the dispute on their own. If no agreement has been reached after 30 days or so, the dissenting stockholder may ask a court to determine the fair value.

5.
Special Problems
Of Closely-Held Corporations

There are several definitions of a closely-held corporation. All revolve around the fact that such enterprises are small—not necessarily in dollar volume but in their number of stockholders. Those stockholders usually know one another quite well.

The first definition puts it this way: A closely-held (or closed, or close) corporation is one in which management and ownership are the same and it is unrealistic to think the judgment of the directors will differ from that of the stockholders.

The second definition is more succinct: A closely-held corporation is one with relatively few shareholders.

Apart from definitions, in practice the shareholders in most closed corporations know each other's business skills because they are in close business contact with each other. In fact, they may all work for the same corporation.

An obvious problem arises from this "family" characteristic. An outsider who buys stock is often unwelcome. He suspects that the stockholders or the incorporators themselves may seek at the outset of the corporation's life to restrict the transfer of stock from one stockholder to another. Conditions may be set up, for example, so that if one shareholder wants to dispose of his stock, he must sell to the other shareholders, with the value of his shares determined on a pre-arranged basis. Or the incorporators seeking to retain full control may sell non-voting participating stock to outsiders they do not want meddling in corporate affairs. Such participating stock may be a type of preferred stock which gives the holder no voting privileges but the right to share with the common stockholders in additional dividend distributions after the common holders have been paid an amount equal to the preferred dividends.

Problem of Valuing Shares

Another problem facing the closed corporation concerns the value of the corporation's shares. It is often realistically impossible to agree on their value, because no public market for the shares exists. This condition is especially hard on minority stockholders who may want to dispose of their interests but cannot find a buyer willing to pay what they think their holdings are worth.

Since it is difficult or impossible to get a market-place value for their shares, some managements have set up formulas for the pricing of stock that changes hands between shareholders. Here are two approaches currently in practice:

● Fix the selling price of the stock on the basis of its book value—the value of all its assets less the amount of all its liabilities. This formula may require the services of an appraiser to give an independent opinion of how much such things as machinery and customer lists are worth.

● Set up a formula that takes company earnings into consideration. The actual book value of many firms does not reflect how profitable they are, and it usually does not assign a realistic value to "good will"—the fact that customers keep coming back regularly. A shareholder who is also a member of management may have contributed a great deal to the building up of the customer lists, and the extent of his contribution may show up only in the amount of profit the company makes each year. A rough rule of thumb says that a closed corporation is worth about five times its annual pre-tax earnings. A company with steadily rising profits would generally be considered worth more than five times earnings, while one with declining earnings might be valued at less.

In a typical buy-out arrangement, the stockholder seeking to sell his shares agrees that they will be valued at five times the average pre-tax earnings per share for the three full years before the one in which he disposes of his interest.

Getting Funds from Outside

Another problem concerns the difficulty of raising outside capital. Investors shy away from a family-owner and operated corporation because of the difficulty they might experience when they try to sell their shares. Unlike the case of shares of public companies which can be readily sold on an established stock exchange, it is usually difficult even to locate individuals who might care to invest in a small closely-held corporation. The investor in a family enterprise—even a profitable family enterprise —generally has a tough time getting out.

It is usually no more difficult for a corporation to borrow from a bank—or to obtain credit from suppliers—than it is for a sole proprietorship or partnership. However, the owner of the closely-held corporation may have to give up one of the main benefits of incorporating—freedom from personal liability—in order to do so. The reason is that the lender or supplier of credit may insist that, as the controlling stockholder of the firm, you agree to take personal responsibility for the loan. If your corporation defaults, you will have to make good.

A bank or supplier that asks you to stand personally behind your corporation's borrowing may grant you the loan or credit if you refuse to do so. Whether or not you can make your refusal stick depends, of course, on the basic strength of your corporation. If yours is an established concern with an acceptable credit rating, you probably will find banks and suppliers willing to make concessions to get your business.

Lending to Your Own Corporation

Instead of borrowing from or selling stock to outsiders when it needs capital, the typical closely-held corporation sometimes borrows from its own stockholders when the need arises. That borrowing could lead to another problem:

The I.R.S. keeps an eye open for loans by stockholders which it says are equity investments and not loans. If you cannot convince it that such is not the case, any amount the corporation pays the stockholder because of the loan is deemed to be a dividend—not interest. And when the "loan" is repaid to the stockholder, the I.R.S. may consider the amount involved as ordinary income and taxable as such.

Thin capitalization gives rise to the I.R.S. calling a loan by a stockholder an equity investment. This is likely to be the case when a corporation is established with an unusually low contribution by common shareholders relative to the amount of capital needed to operate. In one case, a man set up a corporation to buy a fast-food franchise for $35,000, applying only $5,000 toward the purchase of common stock and advancing the remaining $30,000 to the corporation as an interest-paying "loan." His objective, of course, was to take funds out of the corporation in the form of interest with such payments deducted by the corporation as a business expense. The I.R.S. held that the payments he regarded as interest were in fact dividends.

It is also unwise to put too much in the corporation in the form of equity. When you do so, you not only lessen the opportunity to lend money to your corporation but you may also bring closer the day when you will face the risk of an excess accumulation. As is discussed in Chapter 8, your corporation may be penalized if you accumulate more than $150,000 in liquid assets—and that penalty is more likely when it begins with so much equity that it need not borrow to finance expansion, etc.

What is the best ratio to maintain between debt and equity to avoid challenges from the I.R.S.? No one can say with certainty. As a general principle, however, it seems unwise to "lend" more money to your firm at any time than you invest in its stock.

The courts also have their opinions on this point. Here are some of the factors they have considered in deciding when a loan is legitimate and when it is not:

• Is the creditor the only shareholder? If so, the loan will be more suspect than would otherwise be the case.

• Had the corporation been turned down by outside financial institutions when a loan was requested? If so, the loan by the stockholder will appear more legitimate—even a "loan of last resort."

• Is interest at prevailing rates paid on the loan? If so, the loan looks more legitimate than one calling either for little or no interest, or for higher rates than might be obtained elsewhere.

• Is there a fixed maturity date? Such is the typical arrangement for loans made at arms-length. The shorter time the loan runs, the less likely that it will be challenged.

If any loan you yourself make to your corporation is likely to be challenged, consider letting your children become the creditors. That way, if the I.R.S. later calls the loan equity and not a loan, the return of capital in the form of ordinary income will go to the children, whose tax brackets will be low. Of course, you may first have to give your children the money with which to make the loan. With your spouse, you can give each child $6,000 a year free of gift tax. (With your spouse, you may also give away an additional $60,000 free of tax during your lifetime.)

Disposing of a Stock Interest

Still another problem facing the closely-held corporation is what to do with the stock held by a stockholder who dies or retires. Unless an orderly transition of that stock is worked out in advance, the retiring stockholder may lose many of the benefits due him after his service to the corporation.

A sound capital structure for a closed corporation should provide for:

• Redemption of participating stock held by employees after their retirement, disability, or death. The corporation might require an employee to sell his stock back to the corporation. Under a detailed plan, provisions should be made to determine how much each share is worth and precisely how those shares are to be phased out.

• The sale of participating stock to younger key employees.

Here is one example of how securities may be phased out:

When an employee hits age 65—or is permanently disabled—he must divest himself of three-quarters of his stock by selling it to the corporation or to someone the corporation designates with stockholder approval.

Then, when that employee dies, his estate must sell 90 percent of his stock to the corporation.

Finally, when the employee's widow dies, or his youngest child reaches age 21, the remaining 10 percent of the stock must be sold to the corporation.

Using Stock to Attract Outsiders

Most owners of small corporations probably regard the minority stockholder who is not a family member as an ogre seeking to worm his way into their private operation. But there may be a time when you will seek him desperately. For example, you might want:

• To hire an executive away from a competitor. You offer him stock in your corporation so that he will have a piece of the action—an opportunity to share directly in the profits his skills make possible.

• To raise $50,000 or $100,000 now when your local bank is unwilling to lend the money and you have no other way of borrowing it. You must look outside to find an investor willing to put up the needed cash. But he too may be unwilling to lend the money unless he has a chance to make a better profit on it than usual.

• To market a newly developed product with a fantastic potential. At a time when you cannot afford to pay cash for the privilege, you might offer the product's manufacturer or inventor stock in your corporation in exchange for the marketing rights.

In cases like this, you may have to deliberately court the potential minority stockholder. You also must show him that your enterprise will be profitable and that his investment will be greatly enhanced.

When you offer stock in your corporation, however, the potential minority stockholder knows that his will be one small voice speaking out against your loud shout as the major stockholder. He knows that under such circumstances he could be powerless—not an attractive prospect.

Consequently, if you are to succeed in getting him to part with $50,000 to $100,000, say, you will have to protect his interest.

The most common way is to amend your by-laws so that directors (or stockholders if you have not named the minority holder to the board) must reach unanimous decisions on certain actions up for consideration. Otherwise the actions will be rejected out of hand. This provision gives the minority stockholder veto power over some decisions that he might consider detrimental to his interests. While giving him the right to say "no" to certain proposals—a plan to merge with or acquire other companies, say—you will have to be careful not to give away too much power that would, in effect, turn control of the corporation over to him.

The kind of actions that would be candidates for such unanimous approval will vary from minority stockholder to minority stockholder. Each potential investor has his own set of fears, some of which may not always be rational. But you must allay them if you are to get the money, product or executive you want.

Here are examples of the kinds of requests minority stockholders might make:

An executive employee who joined a firm from a large competitor in a major city because of the job challenge and the stock offer that might one day make him wealthy sought 100 percent approval of directors or stockholders before the corporation's headquarters could be moved to another city. He also insisted on always having the right to report directly to the corporation president and to nobody else.

Another executive required the option to buy additional shares each year based on a formula linked to corporate sales or profits or to the sales or profits of his division.

An inventor whose product was to be marketed by a corporation, and who was to be paid in stock, insisted on 100 percent approval of the stockholders or directors before the corporation could lease or rent the product.

Some requests by minority shareholders may seem impertinent. But they reflect the legitimate concern of individuals who are putting their money or their futures, or both, into your hands. They ask for some control of their own destinies.

Note that changes you make to protect the interests of minority stockholders must be clearly spelled out in your corporate by-laws.

The Need for "Corporation Life Insurance"

The success of a closely-held corporation usually rests on one or two persons. If death hits a key executive, the whole operation might be disrupted. At worst, the firm might have to go out of business. At least, a successor will have to be found, hired and trained. In any case, funds will be needed to carry the firm until it can be liquidated in an orderly way, until it can be sold at more than distress prices, or until a new executive can get it running smoothly again.

Other death-related problems arise in the small corporation. The manager is usually the major stockholder and upon his death his stock passes to his heirs. If his estate is large, the heirs may have to sell some of their stock to pay estate taxes. As we have seen, a ready market often does not exist for shares of a small corporation and it may be difficult to find a buyer who will pay what they are worth.

Another problem revolves around the passing of shares into many hands, with no person holding enough to control the corporation. When this happens—as, for instance, when several children inherit a parent's shares—there may be a battle for control while the corporation's fortunes race downhill.

Heirs of a principal stockholder face many serious questions when he dies. Will they want to manage the company, and could they do so competently? Do they have enough money to meet the death costs? If some heirs want to sell their stock immediately, will the others have enough money to buy them out and keep ownership in a few hands? If the heirs continue to hold the stock, will they receive enough income to maintain a suitable standard of living?

Insurance spokesmen say that these questions can be met with a stock sale-and-purchase agreement with life insurance written into it to guarantee the funds for carrying it out. This agreement can determine in advance what will be done upon the death of a major stockholder, and the insurance proceeds make it possible to carry out the plan's objectives.

A typical stock sale-and-purchase plan states what the price per share will be, or it provides for appraisal procedures so that an outside expert can determine a fair price. Both heirs and surviving stockholders are assured of an orderly take-over of the deceased shareholder's interest.

The Life Insurance Institute points out that life insurance can provide the corporation with funds to purchase a dead stockholder's interest at a minimum tax cost. "Where estate taxes are a factor," it says, "the businessman whose holdings of stock in a closed corporation represent 35 percent of the gross value of his estate may have the corporation redeem enough of his stock to cover estate and inheritance taxes without the imposition of ordinary income taxes.

"The benefits of such a plan are many. Continuity of management without interruption is guaranteed. No outsiders can come into the business unless this has been agreed upon in advance.

"The cash needed to carry out the purchase of the stock is automatically provided on a basis previously agreed to as fair. The common causes of friction between heirs and surviving stockholders are removed.

"Widows or heirs are not burdened by business responsibilities or worries. Having a guaranteed buyer and a guaranteed price, they are protected against shrinkage of stock values.

"Not only is the credit position of the firm saved from damage; it is actually enhanced by the plan. The morale of employees is assured for the period of adjustment."

Any stock sale-and-purchase plan must be tailored to the particular situation. It should be in written form, worked out after consultation with the life insurance agent and other experts. It should identify the parties to the agreement and spell out all basic details—who is to become the owner, what stock will be sold, who will receive the proceeds, what life insurance policies will be bought, who will pay the premiums and be the beneficiary of record, and how the stock will be valued (or periodically revalued). A clause in the agreement should bind executors and heirs as well as the stockholder.

Life insurance premiums paid under stock sale-and-purchase agreements are not deductible expenses insofar as income or federal estate taxes are concerned.

The Value of "Keyman Insurance"

It may also be wise to take out insurance on the life of any key employee whose death could result in serious hardship or financial loss to the firm. Such a "keyman" is often a "keywoman"—a secretary, for example, who is responsible for handling many of the firm's details and who might be difficult to replace without a great loss of money and training time. The firm pays the insurance premiums, names itself as beneficiary, and receives the proceeds if the employee dies during the period of coverage.

To decide whether and to what extent to insure an employee's life, estimate the cash cost to you if the employee died. Include possible benefits you might pay the employee's heirs, how much time you would lose in finding and training a replacement, and additional hiring costs—employment agency fees, for example. If the total amounts to only a few hundred dollars, there is no point to insurance. But if the sum totals thousands—and you can ill afford such a loss—the protection is indicated.

According to Treasury regulations, keyman insurance premiums you pay or incur on a life insurance policy covering any officer or employee, or any person financially interested in your business, are not deductible if you yourself are a direct or indirect beneficiary under the policy. However, proceeds from the policy are not taxable either.

Keyman insurance on your own life may be bought and paid for by your corporation. It is not a deductible expense, but it is one way to spend your corporation's cash to avoid running afoul of penalties for excess accumulations. If you hold all or the greater part of the corporation stock, your heirs will benefit from the tax-free proceeds which go to it. As for the present, the additional insurance you carry may enable you to reduce the amounts of premium payments that come out of your personal income.

6.
The Pros and Cons
Of Subchapter "S" Corporations

An interesting possibility for persons who want to incorporate their businesses or professional practices lies in the complex world of Subchapter "S" corporations—a land of great potential tax breaks, but also of potential trouble for those who don't carefully follow the rules.

Most business managers who haven't researched the subject of "S" corporations have at least several misconceptions about them and how they work. Such misconceptions are easy to come by. The world of the "S" corporation is filled with time limits that can't be postponed, regulations, provisos, prohibitions and pitfalls.

What an "S" Corporation Is

A Subchapter "S" corporation is also known as a "pseudo-corporation." It gives you all the protection and fringe benefits you'd get via a real corporation—plus some nice income tax benefits.

This kind of corporation permits you to take most of the tax-deductible fringe benefits available to corporation employees but not to individual business owners or partners. Such fringe benefits include paid hospitalization, life insurance, etc.

And an "S" corporation gives you the same freedom from personal financial liability that the owners of regular corporations get.

The most important feature of the "S" corporation is that it pays no income taxes. Instead, it passes its profits to its shareholders, who pay taxes on the income as private individuals.

Yet, if the "S" corporation suffers a loss, the losses are passed on to stockholders who may apply them against other personal income when filing their own tax returns. (However, no stockholder may deduct as a loss any amount larger than his total investment in the corporation.)

You must distribute those profits to your stockholders within 2½ months after the end of your tax year. If you fail to do so, your stockholders will take a tax beating. Here's why: The I.R.S. will automatically consider all such profits as having been distributed (even though they were not) to the stockholders. They will then be responsible for paying the tax on that income that never came in. Further, the I.R.S. will assume that once the stockholders "received" their money they all turned it back to the corporation as a contribution to capital.

As you can see, an "S" corporation treats you as a corporation in terms of protection and fringe benefits, but in terms of income taxes as a sole proprietorship. It's a good combination for people who qualify.

What It Takes to Qualify

Rules and regulations determine who may and may not become a Subchapter "S" corporation. You must meet them all:

- Your state must permit such corporations. (Most do.)
- Your corporation must be an American corporation, incorporated under the laws of one of the states.
- Your corporation must not be affiliated with other corporations in any way.
- Your corporation must have no more than 15 stockholders. Under a change in the law effective in 1979, a Subchapter S corporation may start out with fewer than 15 and raise the number at any time. Formerly it could have 15 only after operating for five years with no more than ten. When husband and wife own stock as tenants in common or joint tenants or as community property, they're counted as one stockholder. If either husband or wife (but not both) own stock individually as well as jointly, those two individuals don't count as one stockholder.
- Your shareholders cannot be non-resident aliens.
- Your shareholders must be either individuals, the estates of deceased individuals in the process of administration, or grantor, voting or testamentary trusts under certain conditions. In voting trusts each beneficiary is counted as a sep-

arate stockholder. Estates of infants, incompetents and of individuals in bankruptcy or receivership are disqualified.

• Your corporation must have only one class of stock outstanding. That rule is designed to facilitate passing along to the shareholders the corporation's profits, making everyone equal.

In determining whether or not your corporation has one or more classes of stock, consider these guidelines:

Only stock which you have issued and is outstanding meets this qualification. Treasury stock of another class previously issued and later redeemed doesn't enter the picture. Nor does authorized but unissued stock of yet another class. You may get away with two classes of stock, provided they are identical except that each class has the right to elect directors proportionate to the number of shares in the class. Such two classes will be deemed to be one class. Finally, don't be concerned about issuing warrants and options. They won't add another class of stock to your corporation.

If you think you can easily join the ranks of the "S" corporations—but aren't quite sure whether such a corporate structure is to your advantage—consider its drawbacks and advantages.

Drawbacks of "S" Corporations

1. You're limited in the amount you can contribute to your pension fund or profit-sharing plan. In fact, you'll have to live with the Keogh plan which today confines your tax-free contribution to a maximum $7,500 annually. (Many business and professional men find this limitation on pension benefits outweighs any advantages the "S" corporation provides.)

2. You can easily—and unwittingly—lose your "S" corporation status—and incur taxes and fines as well. Consider these relatively easy ways your "S" corporation can be automatically terminated—leaving you defenseless in the eyes of the I.R.S.:

• One of your stockholders transfers his or her shares to a trust or a corporation. That action alone kills your "S" corporation in its tracks.

• Any new stockholder refuses to consent to the Subchapter S election. Formerly, a Subchapter S corporation was disqualified if new shareholders failed to sign a statement agreeing to the election. It's now assumed the new stockholder agrees to it unless he files a formal refusal.

• Stock is accidentally sold to more stockholders than the law permits (up to 15, with husband and wife ownership counted in the way described above). If you take in more than the permitted number, you lose your status then and there.

• Your corporation in one year gets more than 80 percent of its gross receipts from outside the U.S. That heavy emphasis on international funds stops your "S" status instantly.

• Your corporation in one year earns more than 20 percent of its gross receipts from passive income: royalties, rents, dividends, interest, annuities, or profits on the sale of securities. Once you have earned that much passively, you're out of the "S" corporation world and on your own. (However, you may subtract the rentals whenever you can show you provide services for the tenants. Thus, motel and hotel incomes do not count. Nor do apartment house rentals when you give the tenants maid services and the like.)

3. When you lose your "S" corporation status you become subject to additional taxes and penalties. These can mount up year after year until the I.R.S. gets around to auditing your books and uncovers the wrong move you may have made a long time before. (It's possible to continue operating as a Subchapter "S" corporation blithely unaware that its status actually was lost years ago.)

4. You cannot plow back earnings into the "S" corporation—to have money for plant expansion, market research, or what have you. The structuring of the "S" corporation prohibits that salting away for a rainy day.

Advantages of "S" Corporations

• You can draw as large a salary as you wish without fear that the I.R.S. will deem it out of line with comparable salaries in your industry. You can do this because your salary is no longer a tax-deductible expense for your "S" corporation.

• You need not concern yourself about being taxed on accumulated earnings over $150,000. It can't happen to an "S" corporation.

• You can shift income to your children whose tax brackets are low or non-existent. This is an excellent way to save for their college education. But—don't go overboard and draw too small a salary for yourself so your children can draw even more out of the company. The I.R.S. will view the gambit as a device to avoid taxes and force you to give yourself a raise.

- You can afford to launch a new corporation (while running a profitable business elsewhere) because those first- and second-year losses that most new enterprises experience can be subtracted from your profitable activities when filing your tax return.
- You need never worry that you'll be termed a personal holding company subject to extra taxation. Many one-man operations of regular corporations live with that worry daily.

How to Convert to "S" Status

Conversion to Subchapter "S" status is done via an election of all stockholders. Here are the specifics:
- Every one of your stockholders must consent to the conversion. No negative votes are allowed.
- Your stockholders must agree to the new status during an election held at any time during the preceding taxable year in which you want your Subchapter S status to be effective.
- If your business is starting out in Subchapter "S", you must find out precisely when your state says the corporation legally comes into existence. Some say a corporation begins with the filing of articles of incorporation.

If incorporation in your state doesn't begin with filing of the articles, you'll then be bound by the rules of the I.R.S. The I.R.S. says that in the absence of state laws defining when your corporation begins to exist, you'll have to abide by Regulation 1.1372-2. This states that the corporation's first year begins when any one of the following three events occurs:
- When you have shareholders.
- When your corporation acquires assets.
- When your corporation actually begins transacting business.

Any of those activities will "kick off" the corporation's first year.

Knowing when your corporation begins isn't critical as long as you don't engage in any corporate activity or significant corporate planning more than a year before the one in which you first operate under the Subchapter S format. Timing is less critical when you already operate in the regular corporate format but want to shift over.

The stockholder election calls for nothing more than all of your stockholders signing a consent form agreeing to have the corporation operate under Subchapter "S". Stockholders' names and addresses must appear on the form along with their signatures, the number of shares owned, and the dates purchased. It doesn't matter whether you use an individual form for each stockholder or have all sign the same statement on one or two sheets of paper. Note that you don't need consent forms from shareholders who acquire your stock after the election. It's assumed that they agree to the Subchapter S arrangement unless they formally state otherwise.

Stockholder consents are binding and cannot be withdrawn individually. However, all stockholders may vote to terminate the Subchapter "S" corporation. But they cannot terminate the "S" corporation in the same taxable year in which they created it. They'll have to wait at least one year.

Once all stockholders have agreed during the proper time for an election, you must then fill out Form 2553—supplied by the Internal Revenue Service—and return that form with a statement (or the statements) of stockholder consent.

Caution: You *must* return Form 2553 *within* the stated election time. The courts and the I.R.S. are unmovable in this regard. Here are some case histories to help enforce this point on you:

An employee of one manufacturing company deposited an envelope containing Form 2553 and the accompanying consent forms in a mail box in the early evening of the last day for a valid election. Unknown to either the employee or the corporation's officers, the post office made it a practice of postmarking all mail picked up on the evening tour as of 3 a.m. the next day. Thus, the I.R.S. denied "S" corporation status to the manufacturing company on the ground that the postmark set the date of filing Form 2553—not the date the mail was deposited. And consequently the filing was late by one day—sufficient to disqualify the company's request.

In another case, a private postage meter stamp on the envelope containing Form 2553 and the consent forms bore a valid date—in terms of being on time for mailing in Form 2553—but the letter was not received by the I.R.S. until a week later. The I.R.S. ruled that the election was invalid on the ground that the corporation's officers had tampered with the postage metering device so they could record a valid date on the letter—several days after the fact. Had the letter been mailed on the date on the private postage meter sticker, the I.R.S. argued, it would have arrived much sooner.

To stay clear of such mailing pitfalls, send Form 2553 via registered mail. In that case the date on the receipt the post office will issue you when you hand over the letter will act as the legal date for election purposes. That receipt will also stand up in court should the I.R.S. later report it never received your Form 2553.

PROTECTING YOURSELF AGAINST LOSSES

If the complexities of converting your enterprise into a Subchapter "S" corporation are more than you can tolerate, do not automatically assume you have lost the tax-benefits battle. There's yet another way to protect yourself:

Consider going the Section 1244 route. It offers you—from a tax point of view—a "heads I win, tails you lose" deal. And it is not too difficult to qualify.

Section 1244 of the Internal Revenue Code was specifically enacted to aid in the financing of small businesses. It lets you convert what otherwise would be your corporation's capital loss into an ordinary loss deduction—within limits.

As a shareholder in a Section 1244 corporation, you may take as an ordinary loss deduction against personal income corporate losses of up to $50,000 a year — $100,000 on a joint return. (Anything beyond those amounts must be treated as a capital loss.)

To best appreciate what Section 1244 can do for you, bear in mind that if you were operating as a regular corporation, the best you could do with corporate losses would be to deduct them from whatever capital gains you might have. Apart from that, you would be reduced to deducting those losses from your personal income at the snail's pace of $1,000 a year.

This Section doesn't take away the possible benefits of long-term gains. If your corporation does well and you sell your stock at a profit after a one-year holding period, your gains will be taxed at long-term capital gains rates—roughly 40% the usual rates.

Thus you get the best part of both worlds with Section 1244: ordinary losses if the company runs into trouble, capital-gains profits if it prospers.

To put yourself in this favored tax position, your corporation must qualify for Section 1244 treatment. This is what's involved:

• Your corporation must meet the requirements of a "small business corporation." That means all its common stock must be worth less than $1,000,000. There's no longer a requirement that your equity capital (including the stock) must be less than

$1,000,000 when you choose to go the Section 1244 route.

• Your corporation must be an operating enterprise. It must get more than 50 percent of its gross receipts from sources other than royalties, rents, dividends, interest, annuities, and security transactions. In other words, your income must come mostly from the making of a product, the selling of a product at wholesale or retail, or the providing of a service.

• Your directors no longer need adopt a written resolution authorizing the corporation to take advantage of Section 1244. The stock must then be offered under this this Section during a specified period—no longer than two years after the directors have adopted the plan. The plan also should spell out the maximum amount of money the corporation will get for the common stock it issues. The text of a typical resolution, which you may use as your own, is contained in the appendix.

• The directors' resolution to adopt Section 1244 status must be recorded in the corporate minutes. (If a stockholder later claims a loss on his tax return, he should include a copy of the directors' resolution. That's required substantiation to permit the more favorable tax treatment of the loss. Without it, the I.R.S. will not understand you are abiding by the Section 1244 rules.)

• Your Section 1244 stock must be common stock. If other stock is outstanding—including stock rights, warrants, options, convertible securities—such stock must be withdrawn before the plan to issue Section 1244 stock is adopted.

• Corporation, trusts, and estates may not own Section 1244 stock. Only individuals and partnerships may take advantage of the option.

• You must pay for your Section 1244 stock either with money or property.

• You must continue to hold Section 1244 stock for it to be valid. You can neither give the stock away nor sell it. If you do so, that stock will lose its special status.

7.
The Good and Bad
About Professional Corporations

Traditionally, state laws have forbidden corporations to have as their purpose the practice of a profession — law, medicine, dentistry, and so on. Public interest, said the authorities, demanded that persons who obtain a license granted on the basis of their education, skill and character must be regarded individually as "professionals."

Within recent years, however, virtually every state has enacted legislation allowing professionals to form corporations or associations. More importantly, the Treasury Department in 1969 conceded that professionals organized under state professional association acts will generally be taxed as corporations.

This newly developed ability to break into the world where tax benefits abound has prompted tens of thousands of professionals to form corporations. This is especially true of doctors, lawyers, architects, and accountants.

You can enjoy the numerous fringe benefits available to corporation employees — participation in a pension and profit-sharing plan up to $25,000 in tax-sheltered dollars every year as well as company-paid medical, dental and life insurance and all the other well-advertised features that corporations may give their employees. One survey of doctors, asking why they incorporated, put "tax-free pension plans and fringe benefits" at the top of the list. When other doctors were asked why they did *not* incorporate, a majority said they did not earn enough to take advantage of the generous pension and profit-sharing plans that incorporation offered. This survey pointed up the fact that the higher your income, the more appealing incorporation becomes.

Basic Features of Professional Corporations

Despite the fact that many professionals consider incorporation to be one of the best things ever to happen to them financially, there are certain restrictions to operating within this format. Every state has specific regulations covering who may organize a professional corporation and be a shareholder or officer, and the activities in which it may engage.

These are the typical requirements:

● In most states, a professional corporation must be organized for a specific professional purpose — for example, for the practice of medicine, law or other profession involving personal service to the public and requiring that you must be licensed to engage in it. Each state sets its own rules on who may and may not incorporate as a professional. Examples of eligible services include: certified and public accountants; chiropractors, dentists, physicians, surgeons, optometrists, veterinarians, osteopaths, podiatrists, chiropodists, architects, professional engineers, land surveyors, lawyers.

● Only professionals within the same field and same office may form a corporation. All shareholders and directors of the professional corporation must be licensed in that profession. Any employee of the professional corporation who also renders professional services must also be licensed. Office assistants, etc., who help in the management of a professional practice aren't considered to be performing professional services.

● Shares in the professional corporation may be issued or transferred only to a licensed person.

● Stock of a disqualified or deceased shareholder must be bought by the corporation or another licensed professional within 90 days of disqualification or within six months of death. Otherwise the corporation must dissolve.

Plusses and Minuses

There are pronounced advantages to incorporating your professional practice—if you are in a position to make the most of the opportunities it offers. Not everyone is. You should review your specific personal situation with your lawyer, accountant and tax consultant before making any decisions.

In general, here is what incorporating as a professional involves:

● The confidentiality between you, the professional, and your client is *not* lost or abandoned when you form your corporation.

The privilege of total confidentiality has been carried over to the corporate world. State laws typically declare that "nothing in the regulations shall be interpreted to abolish, modify, restrict, limit or alter the law applicable to the professional relationship and liabilities between the person furnishing the professional services and the person receiving such professional service, or the standards of professional conduct applicable to the rendering therein of such services."

• Your professional corporation will not protect shareholders from personal liability. For example, a doctor who incorporates can still be sued for malpractice, and held personally responsible if a judgment is entered against him. This requirement has been built into the rules to safeguard the traditional relationships between the professional and his client, between the professional and his public, and between the professional and other professionals.

• Professional corporations — especially medical ones — usually cannot be formed out of state. They generally must be set up where the individual or individuals perform their services.

• Your corporation's name must contain and must be restricted to the full name or at least the last name of one or more of your shareholders. No impersonal or fictitious names may be used. Many states require that your name also include words such as Personal Corporation (P.C.) to show the world it is dealing with a corporation. (Some states exempt doctors from this requirement.)

• If you establish a corporation in the regular way, you may not take home as high a salary as you did while you were unincorporated. The I.R.S. takes the position that shareholders must receive some benefit from a profitable corporation either in the form of dividends or in the increased value of their investment resulting from earnings retained in the corporation. Of course, before the ordinary corporation may pay dividends or retain earnings, it must pay a tax on its profits. It need not pay a tax on monies paid out in salaries.

A way out of this problem is to set up a Subchapter S corporation — one permitted to pass on all earnings to shareholders free of tax. To qualify as a Subchapter S corporation, certain requirements as to number of shareholders and type of income must be met, as was discussed in the preceding chapter.

• Other corporate costs you've never had as an individual practitioner or partner will also contribute to your lowered take-home pay. Among them are: (1) increased legal and accounting expenses in setting up and continuing the corporate form; (2) paying for the sought-after fringe benefits such as pension plans, key-man insurance, health and accident insurance, group life insurance, etc.; and (3) paying for such mundane expenses as workmen's compensation insurance and unemployment insurance for everyone — yourself included — and not just the clerks and the typists.

● Your professional corporation may not engage in any business other than rendering those professional services for which it was incorporated. But it may own real estate, mortgages, stocks, bonds, or other real or personal property "necessary for, or appropriate or desirable in, the fulfillment or rendering of its professional services," as many states put it.

● Your professional corporation must conduct itself as a corporation — attending to the formalities of directors' and shareholders' meetings, filing of annual reports, abiding by by-laws, and so on.

Here are some specifics: Your by-laws should call for *centralized* management, including control of such matters as the assignment of patients or clients; fixing work deadlines, working hours, fees, salaries, and bonuses; spelling out termination of employment settlements; and the method whereby clients will be selected or rejected.

Moreover, if the corporation includes two or more professionals, you'll need an employment contract with each one — a contract made at arms length, meaning one that does not favor its shareholders inordinately. Finally, the corporate name must be used on your letterheads, bills, office doors, in directories, and in the corporation's bank accounts.

Because of such strictures, you'll do well to gird yourself to working within the somewhat confining structure of a corporation.

● Once you incorporate, you lose your right under the Fifth Amendment to the Constitution which protects individuals against self-incrimination. That means if an IRS agent demands to see the books and records of your professional corporation, you and other professionals who may be within that corporation cannot withhold them on the grounds that those books might tend to incriminate either you or your associates — or both. The reasoning behind that regulation: The protection against self-incrimination is a personal privilege that may not be utilized by a corporation with respect to corporate records.

Incorporating a Group

As a rule, any number of professionals may incorporate. In addition to the benefits of incorporating mentioned above, which apply even if the corporation consists of one person, many professionals find that going in with a group provides these advantages:

• You will be relieved of the pressure you may face while working solo — the fear that your practice might collapse were you to become seriously ill. As one of several members of the corporation, you can relax with the knowledge that others could back you up if prolonged illness kept you from the shop.

• As a group member, you can consult with your peers on knotty problems, benefiting from their experience.

• Your professional corporation can build an independent reputation for itself — something not possible for a solo practitioner. With an established firm name, your group can attract young, well-educated, well-trained professionals as employees.

• Operating expenses are generally lower. The costs of office space, clerical staff, utilities, equipment, etc., are shared by many, rather than one person alone.

Disposing of Corporate Shares

If a stockholder in an incorporated group dies or is disqualified, problems may arise over the disposition of his interest. Since only professionals may be stockholders, stock of the member involved must be either sold to an "outsider" professional or redeemed by the corporation. (Contrary to popular belief, in the event of death, neither executor nor administrator of the estate may become a stockholder in the professional corporation.)

But having to sell the shares is not the rub. Setting the value of the shares is the problem. Some states stipulate that the shares must be sold at book value unless otherwise stated in an agreement among the stockholders. Unfortunately, book value is usually a meaningless term. It reflects the actual value of the tangible assets — not the value of "good will" built up over the years. Consequently, anyone forced to sell at book value usually must take a beating financially.

The best thing to do under such circumstances: Set up a stock redemption agreement when you initially incorporate. Best approach: Have that agreement say the estate must sell and the corporation must buy all of the deceased (or disqualified) professional's stock at a price based on a spelled-out formula — any formula the members of the professional corporation settle on at the outset of their incorporation.

Since such an agreement insists that the corporation buy the shares, it's sensible to insure that the corporation will be in a financial position to carry out its part of the bargain. The most popular — and most obvious — solution is life insurance, taken out by the corporation (and paid for by the corporation) on the lives of each of the professional members. And you'll do well over the years to see that the face amount of such policies reflects accurately the present value of the shares each of you holds in the corporation.

8.
How to Avoid Hazards
That Could Increase Your Tax Bill

In Chapter One, we stressed the advantages and disadvantages of incorporating your business.

Now we will introduce a third aspect into the discussion: Hazards. A hazard is neither an advantage nor a disadvantage. Think of it instead as a navigational obstacle to a boat or a ship: poorly marked channels, rocks, floating debris, shallow water. Such hazards keep the boating enthusiast on the alert because they represent potential danger, but they do not cause him to abandon boating. On the contrary, they instill a respect for what lies ahead and motivate him to learn how to cope.

The tax hazards you will face when you own your corporation are serious. But they won't put you out of business—provided you know they exist and learn how to deal with them.

In this chapter we will discuss the major tax hazards for corporation owners—along with advice on how to get around them for smooth sailing.

HOW TO AVOID "UNREASONABLE ACCUMULATION"

The Internal Revenue Service doesn't like to see a corporation accumulate more money in its treasury than the corporation needs to run the business. The I.R.S. position is so severe that it will impose a tax of 27.5 percent on the first $100,000 accumulated, and 38.5 percent on the excess over $100,000—subject to an accumulated earnings credit. You're allowed to accumulate $150,000 during your corporation's lifetime without facing a penalty. All penalties are levied on amounts above that $150,000.

This penalty is imposed only on earnings for the current year which are retained. It does not apply to a corporation's accumulated earned surplus from prior years. Even if a corporation has $2 million in accumulated earnings, if its current addition this year to earned surplus is $100,000, the tax will be applied to the $100,000 accumulation—not the $2 million.

The I.R.S. maintains that the penalty tax for unreasonable accumulation is one on which a 5 percent negligence penalty can be imposed. This penalty can be added, it says, even though interest on the accumulation penalty tax doesn't begin until notice and demand for payment. The I.R.S. says, however, that whether there is "negligence" will depend on the facts and circumstances in each case. Closely-held corporations such as yours (as opposed to General Motors, Ford, and U.S. Steel) are more apt to wind up with such accumulations. True or not, we know that's an I.R.S. belief, thanks to the freedom of information act which forced the I.R.S. to publish its Agents Manual.

Why is the I.R.S. set against a corporation—particularly a small corporation of which all shares are in a few hands—accumulating earnings beyond a certain stated figure?

Persons who own all or most of the stock of a small corporation frequently find it to their disadvantage to receive dividends because such income can put them in a higher tax bracket. So unless the typical owner of a small corporation really needs the money, he would just as soon not receive the dividends.

On the other hand, the I.R.S. feels cheated if profits are kept in the corporate treasury and not distributed as dividends.

That activity in effect lessens tax revenue for the I.R.S. Hence the accumulation of money by a corporation thwarts its attempt to collect as much tax as possible. (If no dividends are paid, there's no tax due on the dividend income.)

Consequently, I.R.S. agents work hard to see that as much tax is paid (legally, obviously) as possible.

Thus, this penalty tax—called the 531 Penalty Tax—is intended as a deterrent. In effect it says: "OK, Mr. Corporation Owner, if you want to keep that money beyond a certain amount in your treasury that you need to meet the legitimate needs of your business, well and good. But we're going to take between one-quarter and one-third of it from you in taxes. So you would usually be better off if you distributed those dollars to your shareholders."

One tax expert expresses it this way: Section 531 was designed to eliminate the practice of making a controlled corporation an incorporated "pocketbook."

While favoring stockholders who don't want to pay high taxes on dividends, there's another major reason for a corporation to accumulate earnings: Such earnings will raise the value of the corporation's shares. Should you later sell your stock, it will fetch a price that reflects, among other things, the amount of cash in the till. And profits on that sale will be taxed at the capital-gains rate—roughly half the regular rate.

Note that your corporation will *not* automatically be taxed just as soon as it has accumulated money beyond its $150,000 credit. There are legal ways to avoid the penalty. There are also some poorly advised ways to stave it off.

The best of all the ways of proving that you have sound reasons for accumulating the money and are not trying to protect stockholders from additional dividend income is this approach:

Prove you have amassed the money to use for the legitimate needs of the business. That way you are on safe ground and without a doubt will not be subject to the penalty. (But if the I.R.S. has reason to think you're playing games with the accumulated money merely to make it look as though it's intended to be used for the business, it will try to impose the penalty.)

There are specific and legitimate reasons you can have for accumulating large amounts of cash:

• To keep up with your competitors. Let's say that because of technological advances in your industry, you're saving money to invest in more sophisticated equipment.

• To accumulate inventories. (This is especially valid in periods of high inflation when almost everything you use for your business will cost more tomorrow than it does today. Buying in anticipation of rising prices is sound business practice.)

• To expand into a new plant, office, factory, retail store, etc.

• To buy additional machinery or replace old machinery—or both.

• To diversify into other fields because you're now a one- or two-customer business.

• To buy another business.

• To provide for the retirement of bona-fide indebtedness created in connection with your business.

• To provide adequate working capital during periods when you will spend a great deal on inventories, etc., while your receipts are low. See the discussion of the Bardahl Formula below.

• To set up a reserve for pending litigation.

• To set up a reserve for contingent liability under profit-sharing and pension plans.

• To provide funds for pollution control.

• To set up a fund so you can later repurchase your stock.

• To accumulate money to offset a possible loss on the sale of a subsidiary.

There you have a baker's dozen acceptable reasons why you would need to accumulate earnings in your corporate treasury.

"Business Expansion" the Best Reason

Of all the reasons cited, perhaps the soundest are those concerning buying new equipment, plants or office buildings. In short, business expansion.

Many tax experts say you'll never have a tainted accumulation in the eyes of the I.R.S. unless you have an excess of liquid assets—cash, treasury bills or notes, or other securities quickly convertible into cash. If you invest all or most of your profits in bricks and mortar or equipment, you'll obviously use up your liquid assets. And without liquid funds there can be no dividend distribution.

Thanks to such re-investment, you'll be doing what most growth-oriented companies do as a matter of course, irrespective of their shareholders' financial sensibilities. You'll be plowing much of your earnings back into the business so that in the years ahead your earnings will be even greater.

Basically, for profits to grow, the corporation must expand, buy new equipment, stay abreast of the latest technological developments, engage in market research, publicity, advertising, etc.

Whether or not you intend to expand your business or buy new equipment, you can use such reasons for accumulating the excess dollars. But the I.R.S. wants you to show specific and feasible plans that you worked up to expand your business into larger quarters or to buy new equipment.

For example, a Bridgeport, Conn., plastics processor was asked to explain why he had piled up a $218,000 reserve. He said he needed the money to build a new plant. He submitted a deed to a plot of land he had just bought and showed that he had retained an architect to draft plans for the building. In the light of those facts, the I.R.S. agreed that his reserve was not excessive. But after a reasonable period of time—within a few years, normally—you must translate your plans into action. You cannot have unrealized plans to use your funds indefinitely.

The best place to document your plans is in your book of corporate minutes, kept by the secretary who records decisions taken by the directors during their board meetings.

Such plans should also be documented in correspondence between, say, your firm and manufacturers of equipment, between your firm and real-estate agents who would assist in locating new plants or new office facilities, or between your firm and local Chambers of Commerce, who are usually delighted to spell out the benefits of settling in their community.

Obviously, if you have never been in touch with the manufacturer of the $200,000 press you've told the I.R.S. agent you're going to buy, you'll find it difficult to convince him you have been saving to use the money that way.

The same holds true if you've never contacted those real-estate agencies or visited cities at the invitation of the Chamber of Commerce. With such a record you will have a poor case at best.

Here's how one entrepreneur salted away earnings in a legitimate manner that probably no I.R.S. agent would quibble with. He bought a tract of land next to his factory and paved it to provide parking for employees and visitors. He has twice as many parking places as he presently needs. But who can say that his business won't expand in the next few years? Indeed, the time may come when that lot will be too small. But that's conjecture.

The manufacturer confesses that his real purpose is to hold the land for future sale. But his use of it for a parking lot for employees gives him a legitimate business reason for its purchase. In short, he has invested his money in real estate that conforms with his corporation's operation.

Building Cash for Periods of Low Income

Another legitimate reason for accumulating cash in excess of the $150,000 allowance is to keep the company going when receipts will be low. Tax courts have accepted the "Bardahl formula" to determine what these reasonable needs would be. This formula grew out of a tax case involving the Bardahl Manufacturing Co. It was established as a way of measuring the reasonable working capital needs of firms which operate on a seasonal basis—for example, the toy manufacturer who incurs heavy expenses early in the year making products for which he may not be paid until the year's end. This manufacturer will have to accumulate a great deal of cash to finance his operations during periods of high production costs and low income.

Almost all businesses can use the Bardahl formula to some extent, because it rarely happens that business income remains constant every month in the year. Contractors may have to pay for supplies and labor months before they are paid by their customers. Many wholesalers and retailers must buy goods in October which will not be sold until December. Manufacturers must invariably finance "work in progress."

While subject to some sharp criticism, the Bardahl formula is viewed by many tax experts as a significant improvement over older rules of thumb that have been used by the courts.

The earlier rules didn't attempt to measure actual working capital requirements. Rather, they merely developed theoretical standards—such as the acceptance of a current ratio of 2.5 to 1 of current assets to current liabilities—which the court applied across the board to all kinds of corporations with diverse operating methods and financial needs.

The Bardahl formula provides a way to determine the working capital needs on an individual basis. It uses the specific financial data of the corporation under scrutiny at the time.

The formula measures the length of the corporation's operating cycle. Typically, this consists of an inventory turnover cycle plus an accounts receivable turnover cycle.

This two-headed operating cycle is expressed as a decimal part of a year (one-quarter, say). It is then multiplied by the cost of goods sold and operating expenses, less depreciation and income taxes for the year. Result: the allowable working capital accumulation of the corporation at year end.

Here's the formula:

Peak month inventory divided by cost of sales plus peak month accounts receivable divided by net sales equals operating cycle as decimal part of a year times cost of sales plus expenses minus depreciation minus income taxes. Your answer is the allowable accumulation for working needs.

The month when the cash needs of the business will be greatest is that month in which the sum of inventories and accounts receivable is the highest for the year.

Acts That May Trigger a Penalty

Tax court records tell of hundreds of cases in which corporate accumulations were held to be attempts to outflank the law. These are some of the activities which are likely to bring on the penalty tax:

● Lending money to stockholders out of dollars accumulated in excess of the $150,000 limit—especially when the loans are made at low interest rates (or no rate at all).

● Investing in unrelated ventures. (Buying property hundreds of miles from, say, your used-car lot. Obviously, there's no business reason for owning such land. Buying property across the street from your used-car lot would make sense, however.)

● Investing in a company your corporation does not control.

● Making loans to companies you don't own.

Those steps are regarded as actions on the part of the corporation owner to reduce accumulated earnings without a solid business reason.

Other signs will lead the I.R.S. to suspect that your accumulated earnings are being held expressly to avoid paying dividends. They are:

● No history of dividends having been paid to stockholders.

● No outstanding debts that would demand large accumulations.

● Your shareholders are wealthy individuals in high tax brackets.

● There are only a few stockholders—perhaps all related to you.

● Your corporation has a high ratio of current assets to working capital required in the business.

● Your corporation has a high ratio of current assets to total liabilities.

To avoid complications over excess accumulations, remember that you're better off if you put too little capital into your corporation—assuming you could add more later if necessary—rather than too much. A company that starts with a great amount of cash reaches the point of excess unused earnings sooner than one which needs all of its income to finance plant, equipment, material, and other needs of the business.

There's another reason for establishing a small corporation with thin capital. Under certain conditions you can then lend it money needed for expansion. It can deduct the interest it pays on the loan as a business expense. If it starts out with a lot of capital, monies paid to stockholders must generally take the form of dividends and go through the two-tax process.

Stock Market Profits a Problem

What if a corporation's investments (in stocks, etc.) increase so much in value that they put the total assets over the amount that can ordinarily be retained for business purposes? This has been the subject of much wrangling in the tax courts.

Some courts have ruled that if a corporation has gains on stock investments, and it would be hard to dispose of its block without marking down the price substantially, the penalty shouldn't apply. In another case, however, a court held that a corporation with substantial gains on this stock had accumulated amounts beyond its reasonable needs.

At this time, no hard and fast rules seem to apply. But you risk I.R.S. action if you could easily dispose of stock (you have a few thousand shares of a company listed on the New York Exchange, say) and insist on holding on for a better price.

You must also beware of the penalty tax if you liquidate a corporation and fail to distribute the proceeds to the shareholders promptly. A corporation manufacturing doubleknit fabrics accepted an offer to sell its business to another firm. The sale was completed in December, 1968. The selling company kept the proceeds of the sale while its officers considered whether to enter a different line of business. After the corporation filed its tax return for the fiscal year ending May 31 of the following year, the I.R.S. ordered a penalty tax on $308,600 of its earnings.

The case went to court. It recognized that the corporation "was suddenly confronted with the problem of finding another business" and that "some breathing spell should be allowed." But, said the court, "the question is how long is a reasonable spell, not necessarily for the implementation but at least for the development of some plans. Here five months elapsed without any such development. Under the circumstances herein, this period is too long."

From this decision, it's obviously wise to make solid plans concerning the use of excess amounts before the liquidation of the corporation becomes effective. Tax experts usually advise that the extra sums be put to work (or distributed to shareholders) within two months after receipt.

DEFENDING THE SALARY YOU PAY YOURSELF

How much of a shareholder-employee's salary—and that of course includes you—is reasonable and thus tax-deductible by the corporation you own is, in the opinion of some experts, the most frequently litigated question in this field of taxes.

When we speak of "unreasonable" salaries we're talking both of the inordinately high and the unusually low. Of the two extremes, the I.R.S. is usually more concerned with a high salary that seems out of line.

Why does it see red when a shareholder-employee draws what it regards as an excessive salary? The answer is that salaries are tax-deductible to the corporation. The higher the salary, the higher the corporation's expenses. Therefore the lower its reported profits—and the taxes on such profits that the I.R.S. collects.

If the salary is considered by the I.R.S. agent to be too little for the job performed, he may reallocate income from a low-bracket taxpayer (in this case your corporation) to a higher tax-bracket taxpayer (in this case yourself).

The I.R.S. is empowered to determine whether it will treat excess compensation merely as a disguised dividend. As you know, dividend income is a hot potato. The recipient of the dividend may be pushed into a higher tax bracket and may not apply to that income the benefit of the 50 percent maximum tax on earned income. Federal taxes on dividends can be as high as 70 percent.

Hence the major danger facing a corporation owner who pays himself an excess salary is this: That part of the salary which is considered unreasonable by the I.R.S. is not a tax-deductible corporate expense, thereby raising corporate profits and taxes. The excess salary can also be described as a disguised dividend to the shareholder, hitting him with a heavier tax than would apply had it been in the form of ordinary income.

Adding to those problems is this unsettling piece of tax legislation: If the I.R.S. attacks the reasonableness of your salary or that of one of your stockholder-employees, your corporation has the burden of proving that the compensation is reasonable. It's not the other way around.

Because of this factor, the head of a book distribution firm was forced to take a cut in salary when he incorporated. His income from his unincorporated activities had been running at about $35,000 a year. After he incorporated, he put himself on the firm's payroll at $38,000 per year. The corporation showed no profit, and the I.R.S. maintained that no disinterested party who owned a corporation would raise the president's salary and take no profits on his own investment. The salary was cut back to $33,000.

How to Protect Yourself

Let's assume you don't want to pay yourself either too much or too little. You'd like to keep the I.R.S. out of your hair as far as unreasonable salary is concerned. What steps can you take to accomplish that?

• Don't draw out so much in salary that by year's end there are little or no profits left in a business that is obviously making good money.

Particularly suspect is an owner-manager's salary which fluctuates in line with profits. According to the regulations, bonuses are deductible if they are for services actually rendered and—together with regular salaries and other compensation—don't make an "unreasonable" total. When the employee is also the owner, the suspicion often arises that the bonus is intended to withdraw corporate profits without paying a tax on them. It's generally better to avoid paying bonuses to yourself. A regular salary is usually easier to defend against charges of "unreasonableness." If you anticipate a good year, make an employment contract ahead of time that gives you a raise in salary.

• Don't pay a shareholding employee a salary higher than that paid to a non-shareholder employee who does comparable work. A clothing manufacturer had given his son shares of stock annually for 15 years and at age 22 the son held a 20 percent interest in the firm. After graduating from college, he went to work for his father at $15,000 a year and at the end of one year received a $35,000 bonus for "meritorious service." The I.R.S. found that the son had been a shipping room clerk for most of the time and it described the "bonus" as an attempt to pay a dividend while circumventing the tax laws.

• Don't pay a salary to a shareholding employee based in any way on how much stock he owns. According to the I.R.S., "If excessive payments bear a close relationship to stockholdings of officers or employees, it would seem likely that the salaries include a distribution of earnings upon the stock." Also suspect are bonuses related to the number of shares held in the corporation.

• If your own corporation's profits are steadily rising, anticipate its annual earnings and set your own salary a year ahead. Don't wait, as did one Iowa corporation owner, and declare yourself a year-end salary increase. The Iowan paid himself $45,000 a year as a full-time employee of his corporation, then began working only part-time. He paid himself $63,000 a year, although he now did much less work than before. The I.R.S. saw no reason for the extra payment and a tax court said that only $40,000 a year could be paid.

• Try to establish a corporate dividend payment history—even if the payments are small. The I.R.S. holds that the reason shareholders invest in corporations is to get a return. Shareholders in a public corporation would not sit still if its officers drew huge salaries while they got no dividends. The I.R.S. says stockholders in small corporations theoretically should be treated the same—even if the shareholders are the executives themselves.

There's much room for argument over what is a "reasonable salary." I.R.S. spokesmen admit they don't use hard-and-fast guidelines. You probably could "overpay" yourself by $10,000 or so without drawing fire. But if you want to be generous to yourself as an employee, it's best to do so with an employment contract set up well in advance and avoid large bonus payments to yourself. One-year employment contracts give you more flexibility than those for longer terms.

How to Prove You're Worth Your Salary

Let's assume you have played the salary game fair and square. Despite your straightforward approach, an I.R.S. agent is asking you why your salary is so high. What then?

Here are ways to protect yourself against that eventuality:

• Work up a list of your duties and responsibilities.

• Keep a diary, log or engagement book. This should show such things as meetings, business trips and lunches, where held, with whom, and for what purpose. I.R.S. agents are always impressed with diaries kept on a continuing basis which show that you do indeed work hard for the salary you receive.

• Document what your salary was when you worked as an executive for another corporation or company you did not control. (It may well be that your earlier job paid as much as you now get and had fewer responsibilities.)

• Clip and file published job descriptions in the help-wanted columns of your local newspaper when a salary is mentioned.

• Find out whether or not Civil Service rates your job and/or jobs of your other stockholder-employees. Such Civil Service salaries would be excellent benchmarks—if they can be obtained. If so, file them for future reference. (The U.S. Department of Labor also issues statistics on various occupations covering a broad range of work.)

Cases Involving Salaries

These are some recent cases which hinged on reasonable/unreasonable salaries:

A San Diego construction contractor whose corporation averaged $100,000 in profits before taxes paid himself a $60,000 a year salary without questions from the Treasury Department. The corporation had an exceptionally good idea and its profits jumped to $300,000. The contractor then tried to pay himself $150,000 a year and was told he could take only $75,000 as salary.

A Kentucky manufacturer took $8,000 a year in earnings while building his firm's business. When it became profitable, he stopped working a six-day, sixty-hour week and put in only half that time. A tax court ruled that the $15,000 salary he now took was reasonable in view of the sacrifices he had previously made for his business.

Three men set up a New York restaurant as a corporation. One served as manager, another as headwaiter, and the third as chef. In their first year they paid themselves $20,000, $17,000 and $16,000 respectively. As business improved and profits increased, they raised their salaries. The I.R.S. noted that the raises exactly equalled the proportion of stock each man held in the corporation. As a result, the total salaries were now $28,000, $31,000 and $27,000. The pattern led to the I.R.S. conclusion that they were actually paying dividends on their stock under the guise of earnings. Their salary arrangement was disallowed.

A Long Island manufacturer of equipment for swimming pools—president and sole shareholder of his corporation—paid himself a salary of $115,000 out of his firm's total pretax profits of $345,000. When the I.R.S. called him on it, he went to the tax court. He argued that he had built the firm from scratch to one with annual sales of $2,800,000 in a 20-year period. The court agreed that his salary was not excessive in the light of his accomplishments. The I.R.S. said the salary was more than most corporations with similar sales pay their chief executives. The court ruled that this analogy—often used by the I.R.S.—failed to consider particular circumstances.

There are also good precedents for paying yourself a highly generous salary if you have made financial sacrifices for your corporation. A tax court found nothing irregular when the owner of a plastics processing corporation paid himself $24,000—the full amount of his firm's pretax profits—after two years during which he worked 60-hour weeks but took only $11,000 a year.

As we observed above, if the I.R.S. decides that your corporation has paid you an "unreasonable" salary, it creates a situation by which you can be fully taxed as an individual on what you have received, and your corporation is also taxed on the same amount.

You can overcome such double taxation by making an agreement that you will repay your corporation any compensation found to be excessive. If the agreement is carefully worded, you may then take a personal deduction for the overpayment you return to the corporation. In effect, you wipe out one tax.

To pass muster with the tax authorities, your agreement must be in writing. It must be in effect before any salary is paid for the year in which the payment is disallowed. You may not set up the repayment arrangement to cover past compensation. The agreement should be expressed as a contract between you and the corporation, and it should have the binding force of the laws of your state behind it. You could include the agreement in the by-laws of your corporation and have its inclusion noted in the minutes of the corporation. You should have the signing of the agreement witnessed.

Salaries You Pay Others May Also Be Questioned

Deductions your corporation takes for salaries and wages of *any* employees—not just those "related" to it—may be disallowed under certain circumstances. To be deductible, services you pay for must actually be rendered. You may not deduct for everyone you put on your payroll, as a midwestern public relations man learned. His deductions for an aunt were disallowed when the I.R.S. established that she did no work for him and that he had made her an "employee" merely to provide her with support.

Compensation must be reasonable. In 999 out of 1,000 cases,

employee salaries are decided in arms-length negotiations and reflect conditions in the labor market. What the typical employer pays is usually in line with what similar employers pay. When compensation is "unreasonable"—almost always when it is too high—a special relationship usually exists between employer and employee.

Often the overpaid employee is a family member. Putting wives, sons and daughters on the payroll is a favorite way of moving family income into lower tax brackets. This maneuver usually withstands scrutiny when the payments for services performed are roughly in line with prevailing rates elsewhere. However, a tobacco wholesaler brought on the agents after he appointed his 22-year old son just out of college as his "sales manager" over eight experienced salesmen and immediately paid him a higher salary than the others received.

When the I.R.S. says salaries to employees are excessive, a sexual relationship often exists. In one case, a "secretary," drawing $12,000 from a closely-held corporation, showed up at its office once a week and stayed just long enough to pick up her check. An actual secretary, who worked 40 hours a week for $8,000, informed the I.R.S. It disallowed the entire $12,000 deduction.

Obviously, salaries and wages paid for different kinds of work in different lines of activity vary greatly. The I.R.S. defines "reasonable compensation" as "the amount ordinarily paid for like services by like enterprises under like circumstances." In considering whether wages you pay your employees are "reasonable," it considers such factors as these:

- Duties performed by the employee.
- How much responsibility he or she has.
- How complex the business is.
- His or her training and experience in the work involved.
- How much time is spent on the job.
- General living conditions in the locality.
- How much profit the enterprise makes.

PLANNING TO REDUCE ESTATE AND GIFT TAXES

The waters of estate-planning for corporation owners can be treacherous. False moves can make life difficult for your heirs once you're dead. On the other hand, some estate-planning steps will enable you to make life easier for your heirs even while you're running your corporation. Here are some ideas:

• Make your spouse the complete owner of your life insurance policies. If your corporation pays the premiums on an insurance policy on your life, and if you make your spouse the owner of the policy, there will be no taxes on the proceeds when you die. What remains of the proceeds will be taxable at your spouse's death. However, to hold off the government tax collectors, your spouse can set up an irrevocable insurance trust to provide that she (or he) gets the income as long as she lives—along with whatever principal she might need in times of economic stress. Thanks to that irrevocable trust, when your spouse dies the fund will go to your children, who escape estate taxes that would otherwise fall due.

• Name a beneficiary for your pension and profit-sharing plans. If you die before you retire, the money in your plans will be exempt from estate taxes—provided that it is paid to a named beneficiary, either an individual or a trust. So check to see that you have executed a beneficiary designation form.

• Rather than name an individual for your pension and profit-sharing plans (your wife, for example), name a trust as beneficiary, providing that income be paid to your wife. At the same time, allow the trustee to dip into principal if your wife needs the money.

(In the past, many trustees and money managers frowned on dipping into capital. But with inflation rampant, there is no certainty that an allotment of, say, $3,000 a month will be sufficient to support your wife and children in 1990. Thus the advice that the wife, through the trustee, have access to capital.)

Thanks to this setup, when your wife dies the money from the trust will be paid to the children without a cent being taxed.

But heed this caution: Put a specific prohibition in your trust agreement that no proceeds from the pension and/or profit-sharing plans will be used to pay estate taxes or claims of the estate's creditors. Without that prohibition, much of the money could become taxable.

• If your corporation is practically a one-man operation, provide for others (your wife, a close business associate) to carry it on without interruption should you die. For example, if nobody but yourself has the right to sign checks, think of how quickly your business would come to a standstill until a probate judge decided to permit your executor to take over. Give your wife—or someone else you trust—the authority to sign corporate checks.

Name another individual to act with you as trustee of your pension and profit-sharing plans. Name your wife or another person an officer in your corporation so he or she will have the right to continue operations.

• Divide your common stock into two classes: Make 10 percent of it Class "A" voting stock and 90% Class "B" non-voting stock. Entitle both classes to receive equal dividends. Then give the Class "B" non-voting stock to your minor children. You still hold all the voting stock. Hence you continue to control your company even though you hold few shares of the total stock outstanding.

Each year distribute a relatively large dividend. Since the children are minors, they will be in a low tax bracket and won't be heavily taxed.

You may have to pay a gift tax when you hand out that non-voting common to your children; but the transfer can be arranged to take full advantage of the annual exclusion ($3,000 which you can give each child each year) so that a minimum tax will be payable.

• Also use the voting/non-voting common when you want all your children to receive dividends but you want only one child to control the corporation one day. Give your successor the voting common and give only non-voting common to the other children. All share in the profits via dividends payable on both voting and non-voting stock.

• Take some of the value of your corporation's common stock and convert it to preferred stock in an amount sufficient to produce, on a reasonable dividend basis, the annual income desired.

Example: Preferred stock with a par value of $12,000 and an annual dividend rate of 7 percent could produce $840 a year cash income to the preferred stockholder. (Preferred stockholders must receive their dividends before dividends can be paid to the holders of common stock.)

Over the years, as you convert common into preferred stock for your heirs, you can slowly reduce the value of your taxable estate.

Say your corporation is legitimately valued at $500,000. Over a period of years you might issue preferred stock with a par value of $500,000 and eventually leave your common stock with no apparent value.

What do you do with the common? You can keep it—and because it alone has voting rights, you retain control over your corporation even as you reduce your taxable estate to a minimum.

• Insert a $5,000 death-benefit clause in your employment contract to exempt payments from both estate and income taxes. (Many employment contracts omit this critical clause.)

• Avoid an insurance-funded stock-purchase agreement. Here's why: Your family members will face an estate tax on the money they get under such an agreement. Instead, have the corporation pay your heirs exactly what their stock is worth at the time of your death—normally the depreciated value of the assets plus any cash on the date the stock is evaluated.

If you have a pension plan that includes the right to payments from the corporation after you leave, there's no way to avoid taxation on the payments to your estate. But if you're setting up a trust anyway, have the benefits paid to the trust so there won't be a second tax when your beneficiary dies.

Using Preferred Stock to Transfer Control

Using preferred stock is also a good way of transferring control of your firm to another person—perhaps your child—while you continue to participate in its profits. You could issue preferred stock to yourself and/or your spouse with regular dividend payments assured. You could also arrange matters so that if the dividends are not forthcoming, the preferred stock gets enough voting rights to outvote the outstanding common stock.

Say you want your son to take over your company now, and to inherit your interest in it upon your death and that of your spouse. You give him the common stock with voting rights while you take only the preferred stock. According to an I.R.S. ruling, you can switch your holdings from common to preferred without paying any tax if the market value of the latter doesn't exceed that of the common you have given up. If the common stock given your son has a proved value (a result of the fact that your new preferred stock is not as valuable as your old common stock) it represents a gift from you to him. A gift tax may be payable to the extent that the common stock's value exceeds the permissible tax-free gifts you can make over a lifetime and during any one year. Upon your death and that of your spouse, your son inherits the preferred stock and may cancel it or exchange it for common stock.

The use of the preferred stock device is obviously one way to retire from your firm while continuing to enjoy income from it. To convince the I.R.S. that you're entitled to tax-free treatment when you make the stock deal, you should have a formal, independent appraisal made of the value of each class of stock.

Difficulties in Valuing a Corporation's Worth

When your stock in a closely-held corporation is valued for death tax purposes, the taxing authorities may hold widely different ideas from your own. Some tax courts appraise the worth of each share according to book value (total assets of the corporation minus liabilities, divided by number of its shares). Others arbitrarily decide what the firm's "good will" and/or earning power are worth. They then assign a discount to allow for the fact that it is difficult to sell shares in a closely-held corporation for their worth on paper. No specific formulas cover how large a discount will be allowed. The iffy nature of valuing such shares means that your heirs should have enough cash to pay the highest tax that might be imposed.

If you own a corporation, see that your heirs won't have to sell their stock at distress prices in order to pay estate taxes. It's usually difficult to sell shares in small corporations. Owners of firms that are large enough often go public when they're ready to retire. They sell enough shares to outsiders to provide the cash needed for taxes.

Owners of smaller corporations often take out life insurance policies for the same purpose. Sometimes a corporation has enough cash (or assets easily convertible into cash) to buy out stockholders who need money. Often shareholders in small corporations sign agreements to sell their shares only to other stockholders according to prearranged formulas. Frequently it's agreed that the value per share will be determined by an outside appraiser.

9.
Tax Strategies to Use
In Operating Your Corporation

The first tax decision facing you as you start your corporation is this: Which of three possible tax years should you select?

Here are the alternatives:

• **Calendar year.** You can select this tax year with no difficulty. There are no requirements. The calendar year—January 1 to December 31—has certain conveniences. For instance, you will never get confused when talking about it. You always know what year it is. But if you select a fiscal tax year, you will be talking about several months in one year and other months in a second year. Fiscal years always occupy portions of two calendar years.

You are free to select a calendar year basis. You *must* accept this basis if you keep no books and have no annual accounting period, or if your accounting period is not a calendar year but does not qualify for fiscal year treatment.

• **Fiscal year.** A fiscal year is any 12-month period ending on the last day of any month except December. It always straddles two calendar years. You may select a fiscal year only when you meet three stipulations: You keep books, you have definitely established a specific fiscal year before the close of your first fiscal year, and your books are kept in accordance with that fiscal year.

• **52-53 week year.** This taxable year is a special type of fiscal year, varying from 52 to 53 weeks and always ending on the same day of the week. This tax year (used by many retailers) can be used only when you keep books, regularly compute your income on a 52-53 week basis, and keep your books on that 52-53 week basis.

Choosing a Tax Year

If yours is a seasonal business, do not pick a fiscal year that splits your busy season into two different taxable years or places the bulk of your receipts and expenses in two different taxable years. To do so is to distort your annual income.

Further, if you operate a seasonal business, bear in mind that your corporation's first fiscal year need not run for an entire 12 months. If you choose, you can cut the first fiscal year to any number of months, or even to one month. (Profits or losses during that less-than-12-month "year" will be treated by the I.R.S. as the entire profit or loss for that "year.")

The option of deciding when the corporate fiscal year ends is a decided advantage for seasonal businesses. You can end the first year so that your anticipated high-income season takes place during your second year. Thus you can postpone tax payments on your first season's income as long as possible. And you can use those tax funds as working capital.

Even non-seasonal corporations can benefit from that first custom-tailored fiscal year. For example, if your net profits are getting close to the point at which taxes on corporate profits increase sharply, you can stop that year on a dime. Thus, you can keep your first year's taxes down to 20 or 21 percent on the first $25,000 or $50,000 of profits—depending upon the tax rates fixed by Congress.

There is still another benefit in choosing the fiscal year. Most small corporations in start-up situations (not those set up to carry on an existing sole proprietorship or partnership) lose money in the first year or two or—at best—manage to about break even.

So if you start your business on August 1, say, chances are good that by December 31, you will still be in red ink. You will have incurred large start-up expenses that stand little chance of being wiped out by income in such a short time. If you chose a calendar tax year, you would have a loss. But if you operate on a fiscal year basis, your business which began on August 1 would not have to end until the following July 31. Obviously, the fiscal year gives your corporation "breathing space"—a time to get on its feet and possibly show a small profit before the tax year ends.

It is easy to adopt any convenient tax year for your new corporation. You need no permission to adopt a short fiscal year for the first year. But it is difficult to change your tax year. You will then need I.R.S. permission. The I.R.S. insists on a formal application—in triplicate, using Form 1228—showing, among other things, that you have a substantial business purpose for the change. And it will want reassurances that any tax advantage resulting from the change will not be significant.

DEALINGS BETWEEN YOU AND YOUR CORPORATION

Most expenses your corporation incurs in the ordinary conduct of its business can be deducted in full on its tax return. The requirements are easy to meet. The expenses must be "ordinary" and "necessary" and also "reasonable." You generally have great leeway in determining how to spend money with the ultimate hope of making a profit.

The requirements stiffen, however, when your corporation engages in business transactions with a "related taxpayer." The I.R.S. then takes the position that you may not be motivated solely by business considerations. It is likely to suspect that in buying or borrowing from, or selling or lending to, a related taxpayer, your objective is to make a gift in the guise of a business expense.

For most tax purposes, you are "related" to your corporation if you and/or members of your immediate family own more than 50 percent of the value of the outstanding stock either directly or indirectly. Members of your immediate family are parents and grandparents, children and grandchildren, husband or wife and—except in some tax circumstances—brothers and sisters. You may also be related if you and/or members of your immediate family control a trust whose stockholdings, along with those of yourself and your family, add up to more than 50 percent of the value of shares outstanding.

In practice, most persons who control more than 50 percent of a corporation's shares fit the description of related taxpayer.

Dealings between related taxpayers usually involve no complications if transacted at arms length—under the same terms that would prevail if parties to the transaction were not related to each other in any way. These are some of the major precautions you should observe:

• You may put your relatives on your payroll, of course, and the owners of thousands of firms do so. All the law requires—if you take a deduction as a business expense for the money you pay—is that compensation be "reasonable" in the light of all circumstances. There is generally no difficulty with the I.R.S. if the amounts you pay related taxpayers are reasonably in line with what you would pay an unrelated employee for similar work. (As a practical matter, a return is more likely to be questioned if the relative is paid more than other people doing the same kind of work, rather than if he is paid the same as others for doing less work.)

The jobs your relatives hold should also be those they are fitted for by experience or education. A construction contractor put his 22-year-old on his payroll as a "liaison" man with vague duties and paid him $25,000 a year while foremen with years of experience earned $10,000 a year less. The son's compensation was ruled excessive by 60 percent because nothing in his background justified the salary. The fact that the son could not have obtained such a high-paying job in the open market was also a factor.

You are subject to being overruled if you take a deduction for compensation paid *anyone* which the I.R.S. deems "unreasonable." But whereas the Service might tend to think your overpaying of outsiders stems from bad business judgment, it usually scrutinizes motives more thoroughly when compensation paid relatives seems unreasonable.

● If you own and manage a closely held corporation, you may have to answer questions if you pay a family member a higher salary than you yourself receive. This is sometimes a temptation for individuals with substantial income from other sources. They may want to limit their own salaries so as to keep their overall taxes low. The owner of a wholesale stationery firm with an independent income from apartment houses paid himself only $15,000 a year as head of the firm over a long period, then installed his son as manager at a salary of $30,000. The I.R.S. allowed a deduction for only $13,000 of this amount and said the rest had to be considered as a gift.

● A related taxpayer may not take advantage of the fixed per diem allowance for travel. Ordinarily, an employee traveling on business may receive $44 a day, or the maximum per diem permitted federal employees in the locality, if the elements of time, place and business purpose of the travel are properly substantiated. It is not necessary to list such items as the cost of food and lodging, etc. But when the employee is related to the employer (owns the corporation that employs him, for example) he must substantiate all the deductions he claims. In effect, the automatic allowance no longer applies.

● If your firm leases property owned by a related taxpayer,

you must deduct the cost of repairs in a different fashion than if the landlord were unrelated. In ordinary circumstances, you deduct the cost of repairs to business property in the year in which you pay or incur them, depending upon the bookkeeping method you use. But if your corporation and the lessor are related, the cost of any improvement may not be recovered over a period less than the remaining useful life of the improvement. This regulation aims to prevent a corporation from deducting the cost of substantial repairs, then moving out and leaving the related owner with property on which higher rents can be charged or which can be sold at a profit taxed at a lower capital gains rate.

• You may be denied the investment tax credit if you buy equipment from a related taxpayer for use in your business. In a recent case a corporation bought a used car from the owner's son when the latter was called to active duty in the Army Reserve. Ordinarily an investment tax credit can be taken for an automobile bought for business use with a useful life of three years or longer. But under the Code of Federal Regulations, the car was not "purchased" from the family member and hence not entitled to the credit.

• You generally have to be careful whenever goods are sold by and to related taxpayers. When there are two or more related taxpayers in different tax brackets, the I.R.S. suspects that income may be shifted from one to the other for tax considerations rather than legitimate business reasons. When large transactions are involved, you would be wise to keep some record showing that the price paid for the goods or services equals the price in an ordinary transaction between strangers.

• If your corporation uses the accrual method of bookkeeping, by which you report transactions when contracted rather than when money actually changes hands, you may not be allowed a deduction for unpaid business expenses or interest your corporation owes to you or another related taxpayer. The exceptions are when the related taxpayer also uses the accrual method, or uses the cash method and receives the money within 2½ months after the close of his tax year. The purpose of this regulation is to prevent a taxpayer from taking deductions for sums not promptly reported by his "relation" as income.

• Accrual method payers which owe money to employees at the end of a tax year ordinarily may not deduct amounts owed related taxpayers unless the payment also is made within 2½ months thereafter.

● Except when a corporation is being liquidated, losses from the sale or exchange of property between related taxpayers is not allowed. This regulation clearly intends to prevent bargain sales on which the seller later reports a loss for tax purposes. It is strictly applied even when the loss is beyond question. In an extreme instance, one taxpayer sold 300 shares of stock through a member firm of the stock exchange. Around the same time, a related taxpayer bought shares of the same company through another broker. The first man did not know who was buying and the second man did not know who was selling. Yet the ban against a deduction on the loss was upheld.

Under the law, the I.R.S. may reallocate income and deductions if it thinks reported transactions between related taxpayers differ from what they would be in arms-length encounters. Especially suspect are rent that a corporation pays its controlling stockholder, and wages paid to a corporation owner's immediate family.

In the I.R.S. view, "excessive rent" which controlling shareholders pay themselves as owners of the building their corporation occupies is a way by which they seek to take disguised dividends out of the firm. Some tax practitioners believe the excesses must be flagrant before the I.R.S. will challenge them. In fact, there are sound arguments for holding that a corporation should pay a somewhat higher rent to a relative, because the tenant generally has the assurance that it will receive first consideration when its lease must be renewed.

In a typical allocation case, two Georgia corporations were owned by the same man. One made low-cost loans to the other at no interest. The second corporation, in a low tax bracket, used the borrowed funds to earn money it could not have earned had it paid prevailing interest rates. The Service decided on its own that the borrower should have paid higher interest. It taxed the first corporation as though it had actually received the interest as income.

TAX MANEUVERS AT YEAR-END

In the last months of your first year's operation, you should determine whether it is to your advantage to lower or raise your income for the particular year. This decision is important because what you choose to do will raise or lower your tax bill.

If you choose to lower your corporate profits and consequently lower your income taxes, you can increase your expenses and defer at least some income toward the close of the year.

It is easy enough to increase expenses so that they fall into one year instead of another. Some examples:

• Pay on the spot for products and services you buy in November and December.

• Pre-pay interest on a corporate loan—up to a year's worth, but not to the extent that you "materially distort" your income.

• Stock up on supplies in December, and pay for them before year's end if you are a "cash basis" taxpayer. (In an inflationary period, such advance buying will get you a lower price than one you might pay several months later.) The absence of ready cash need not get in your way if you want to pay as many bills as possible to build up expenses. Consider taking out a bank loan for 90 days. You can pre-pay the interest in the current tax year—still further hiking your expenses.

To defer income:

• Hold off mailing some or all November bills until mid-December, and offer no inducement for early payments. While it often makes tax sense to hold off sending out bills so that payment will be received after your new tax year starts, get the money now and forget tax considerations if you have any doubts about ultimately collecting from a customer.

• Sell on consignment.

• Sell on approval with the right of return instead of outright sale.

• Sell on installments.

Before seeking to increase expenses and defer income, all with an eye toward lowering your taxes, you should consider this major question: Should you cut your profits?

Yes, if your profits are so high some of those earnings are subject to the higher corporate tax.

Yes, even if your profits are not high—provided there is a good chance that Congress will lower taxes in the next year.

No, if your corporation is a Subchapter "S" corporation and you need every dime you can get your hands on.

No, if profits are so low you will be unable to draw your November and December salaries if you pay out additional dollars in other expenses you do not really need to incur.

No, when you urgently need all the cash you can get.

How to Show Higher Profits for a Year

If you want to show higher profits for any given year, you must cut down on expenses and try to get paid by every customer before your tax year's end.

It is not difficult to defer expenses and step up collections so as to increase your corporation's taxable income. Here are some ways:

- Do not pay November and December bills until January.
- Buy no supplies or equipment you do not absolutely need.
- Step up collections on delinquent accounts.
- Send out your bills promptly. Call debtors and ask for immediate payment.
- Establish lay-away plans.
- Ask for larger down payments when you make installment sales.
- Sell nothing on consignment. Try to get paid for goods and services upon delivery.

Why should you want to increase income and thus income taxes if you show a profit? The answer depends on your personal situation. Here are some yardsticks:

Yes, if you are going to show a loss for the year anyway.

Yes, if you believe Congress will raise taxes next year or that you will be in a higher tax bracket.

Yes, if you need to keep your stockholders happy by distributing a dividend. (Many stockholders do not consider an investment worthwhile—and perhaps rightly so—unless they receive dividends. Why else invest in your corporation?)

Yes, if one or more of your minor children are substantial stockholders who are in a bottom-rung bracket and therefore will pay little or no taxes on the dividends they receive.

Yes, if you want to impress potential investors with your business savvy during your first year or two. A heavy emphasis on collections may not only increase profits but will also make you look good in the eyes of present or potential stockholders. They may not look into all the bills that will have to be faced in the new year.

Accounting Method May Be Crucial

Before you can use the strategies outlined, you should understand that your accounting method will determine what you may and may not do in terms of raising or lowering expenses, raising or lowering income.

There are two approaches to accounting: cash and accrual.

● Cash Basis. If you are on a cash basis, you may legally say, "I didn't earn that dollar today because it wasn't paid to me today—even though I did the work for it." Say a painting contractor paints a man's house in August of this year and the customer does not pay the $2,000 for the job until next January. The painter need not include that $2,000 on his tax return for this year.

From an expense viewpoint, anyone on a cash basis can also say, "I didn't pay for the supplies I received today, so it's not an expense today." Suppose you buy two typewriters at $500 each in December of this year. You do not pay for them until January of next year. That $1,000 typewriter expense is included in next year's tax return—not this year's.

● Accrual Basis. When you are on the accrual basis, you must consider your earnings this way: "I sold the product or did the work today—so I earned the money today even though it wasn't actually paid to me today." To return to the example of painting the house, the painting contractor using the accrual basis would report $2,000 as income for this year, even though he is not paid until next year.

When you are on an accrual basis, you must also consider all expenses as incurred in the year the work was done or the product was given to you. The year in which you pay for the product or service has no bearing. Therefore, in the case of the purchase of the typewriters, you would have had a $1,000 expense on this year's return, even though you do not actually pay until the next tax year.

If you are on an accrual basis, you do not need to hold off billing your customers. The I.R.S. assumes you have been paid. Also, if you are on an accrual basis, you will not need to take out bank loans to make November and December payments on purchases you have built up in order to obtain tax credit for them. The I.R.S. will consider such bills paid on the spot. Under the accrual basis, you can order as much equipment and supplies as you like, deducting the cost in the current tax year even though you pay in the following tax year.

Anyone may elect to use the accrual basis, but you must use it if inventories play an important role in your business. Most manufacturers, wholesalers and retailers must use it.

If you are on a cash basis, you must also be aware of I.R.S. rules about "constructive receipt." That means you must report as income for this year any money that you could put your hands on if you really wanted to. For instance, if you got a check on December 31, and it was a business day, you could cash or deposit it even if you did not do so. That means you may not hold off cashing the check in January and including the income in the next year's taxes. (If you cash the check in January, you are expected to consider the money as having been received in December.)

If a client or customer tells you in December that he has a check waiting for you and you need only stop by his office to pick it up, the I.R.S. also views that situation as constructive receipt. It is income received in December even if you do not pick up the check until January.

LOWERING TAXES VIA INVESTMENT CREDITS

A good opportunity to cut your tax bill comes through the use of investment credits. These are the credits allowed by the government when you buy most kinds of business equipment. They are designed to encourage you to invest more in your business and thus to help the nation's economy.

These are the basic points about the tax credit:

• The tax law of 1978 permanently fixed the investment credit allowance at 10 percent of the investment that qualifies. If you buy a $10,000 item that qualifies fully for the credit (see below) you can cut your tax bill by $1,000.

• You may deduct the amount of the credit from the total tax due on your return. A tax credit is therefore worth more to you than a deduction for the same amount.

• The credit is taken for the year in which you place the equipment in service. It is desirable to anticipate your needs and to take delivery before the end of a tax year in order to get an immediate tax reduction.

• There is a limit to the total credit you can take. Ordinarily, you may not take a credit for more than the amount of your tax liability for the year. As of this writing, your credit is limited to $25,000 plus 50 percent of your tax liability over $25,000 in the case of new purchases. You may count no more than $50,000 worth of used property in any one year for purposes of the investment credit.

• The credit has nothing to do with depreciation, which is

discussed in the section below. You may take the credit and also write off the cost of your equipment as you use it and it decreases in value.

Most equipment you use in your business could qualify for the credit. To qualify, property must be tangible personal property subject to depreciation. This includes all kinds of machinery, office files and equipment, individual air conditioner units, automobiles used in business entirely or partially, etc. It does not include land and land improvements such as buildings, plumbing and heating systems, central air conditioning units, parking lots, etc. Nor does the credit apply to goods you purchase for resale or use in making a product or performing a service.

You can get the credit when you rehabilitate or reconstruct a commercial or industrial building that's at least 20 years old or convert an old residential building to commercial or industrial use.

How Credits Are Determined

The amount of credit you may take depends upon how long the property is expected to last and whether it is new or used. Your first step is to determine the estimated useful life of the property involved. This figure depends to a large extent upon individual circumstances: how often the equipment is used, how well you maintain it, climatic conditions, etc. However, the Internal Revenue Service has prepared guidelines showing estimated useful lives of different kinds of property based upon general experience. Unless your own experience is different, you can use these estimates as a base. They show, for example, that office furniture and equipment like typewriters, calculating machines and photo copiers have useful lifetimes of from 8 to 12 years; automobiles in steady business use stand up for 2½ to 3½ years; and light general-purpose trucks on the road every business day generally last 3 to 5 years.

After determining how long you expect the item to last, you can compute what tax credit you can take. If the property has a useful life of less than 3 years, you may take no credit at all. If it has a useful life of from 3 to 5 years, you are entitled to a credit amounting to 10 percent of one-third of your investment. If the useful life is at least 5 years but less than 7 years, you may take a credit amounting to 10 percent of two-thirds of your investment. If the item is expected to be useful to you at least 7 years, you're entitled—at the prevailing rate when this was written—to a credit of

10 percent of the full amount of your investment.

Say you buy business machinery for $6,000 and expect it to last eight years. You get a $600 credit—the full 10 percent of the purchase price. If you expect its useful life to be six years, your credit drops to $400 (10 percent of two-thirds of the price.) If it is likely to be useful for four years, your credit amounts to $200.

To compute your tax credit on used property, you count only the cost of "qualifying" property bought during the tax year. Suppose you trade in an old machine for another used machine. You count only the additional amount you spend in the trade. Or suppose you sell your older machine and contract, sixty days before or after the sale, to buy a replacement. For tax credit purposes, you consider your cost of the replacement as the price you paid minus what you received on the sale of the older equipment.

As examples, say you see a used machine priced at $5,000 which you want to buy. You have a similar but older machine which you could sell for $2,000 fifty-nine days before you buy (or contract to buy) the replacement. Your investment, for tax credit purposes, is only $3,000. If you trade in the machine and get a $2,000 allowance, your investment also is only $3,000.

You may take a credit for items like automobiles which are used partly for business and partly for personal purposes. In such cases you determine how much you use the equipment in your profession or trade. That percentage of the purchase price becomes your base.

Say you buy a car for $5,000. Past experience tells you you will drive the car 15,000 miles each year for business and 5,000 miles for personal purposes. Seventy-five percent of the cost—$3,750—may therefore be considered for the credit. To determine the exact credit you may take, you estimate the total useful life of the car and arrive at the percentage of the cost you will be allowed. You take this percentage of $3,750. Say a car has four years of useful life to you. Your credit will amount to $125—10 percent of one-third of your investment.

When You Lease Property

Ordinarily you are not allowed to take investment credits when you lease property instead of buying it outright. However, when the property is new and qualifies in other respects, you may take the credit IF the owner elects to pass it on to you. This is a good point to remember when you lease machinery or other items. The value of the investment credit often is not considered when business owners negotiate leasing terms, but in the case of major equipment it could total hundreds of dollars.

The regulations state that the lessor must signify that he is turning the credit over to you on or before the due date of your tax return for the year in which the property is leased. This election is made by filing a statement with the required information signed by lessor and lessee.

As a rule, the lessee signing a long-term lease can get a larger tax credit than the lessor. The reason is that the outright purchaser of equipment uses his cost price to determine the amount of his tax credit. But the lessee computes his credit on the fair market value, which is generally higher. Say an equipment dealer buys a machine at the wholesale price of $6,000 but its fair retail value is $10,000. He is entitled to a credit on $6,000, but the person who leases the machine on a lifetime basis is entitled to one on $10,000.

To get the full credit, the lessee must lease the equipment for the expected useful life of the property. If the term of the lease is significantly shorter than the estimated useful life of the property, the investment credit you could take is reduced according to a formula so involved that it is not usually worth the trouble.

Carrying Credits to Other Years

Do you lose the investment credit if you have no taxes against which to apply it? Many persons who set up businesses take losses at the very time they are buying equipment that would qualify for credit. The law permits you to carry over and carry back your unused credits. Hence you can take advantage of them in your profitable years.

A credit unused for any reason (if you exceed the amount permitted in any year or if you have no taxes against which to apply it) can be carried over to seven succeeding tax years or back to three preceding years. You must use your credit in the earliest year possible.

Suppose you are entitled to a credit this year but cannot use it because you show a loss on your operations. You file your claim for a refund of a preceding year's taxes by filing an amended tax return or by filing a simpler form—Form 1040X, Form 843— specifically designed for the purpose. If you intend to carry your credit forward to succeeding years, be sure to make your claim for it on this year's tax return.

You are expected to maintain records that substantiate your claim if you are questioned by the I.R.S. For major equipment, your records should show the month and year in which you bought the property, the price paid, trade-in or other allowances, and when you put the property into service. When you dispose of the property, keep records showing the date of disposition and amount received for it, if any. You need not keep individual records for "mass assets"—items like electric tools and hardware for which a credit may be taken but which do not involve large sums when taken separately. You are permitted to lump such items together, give them an average "useful life," and account for them as though they were one item.

Other Investment Credit Angles

• If you dispose of your property before the end of its "useful life," you come up against a "recapture rule." You report that fact on your tax return for the year in which you dispose of the property. You also recompute your credit, basing it on the actual useful life of the property—the period beginning with the first day of the month you placed it in service and ending with the date you disposed of it. You then deduct the amount of your adjusted credit from the credit already taken. You pay the balance to the I.R.S. or apply it against other credits to which you are entitled.

• You "dispose" of your property for tax purposes not only when you sell it but also when you give it away, convert it to nonbusiness use, or otherwise cease to have possession of it. However, you are not regarded as having made a disposition if you change your form of operation and retain a substantial interest in your business. For example, you do not lose your credit if you liquidate your corporation and continue to use your equipment.

• If the property in question is stolen or accidentally destroyed before the end of its estimated useful life, you consider it as having been "prematurely" disposed of. You will have to pay the balance due to the I.R.S. When you buy property to replace the stolen or destroyed item, however, you are entitled to use the full purchase price as your basis for determining the amount of your credit.

TAX-WISE DEPRECIATION STRATEGIES

Corporation owners who keep on top of the tax laws almost always are sharp about depreciation as well as investment tax credits. When they spend a dollar for plant, equipment or other depreciable assets, they usually want to deduct its cost in the fastest possible way so that the tax dollars saved can be reinvested in their business.

One way to recover monies spent this way is by accelerated depreciation methods which permit extra deductions during the early years of the life of the asset. You can also speed up your write-off by assigning a shorter useful life to the asset involved—in effect, reducing the number of years over which depreciation will occur.

Under the basic depreciation procedure, you are required to determine how long the asset will be useful in your business—the same figure you use for investment credit purposes. You then determine its "salvage value"—its worth at the end of that period. If the salvage value is estimated to be 10 percent or less of the cost of property with a useful life of three years or more, you can ignore it and base your depreciation on the full purchase price. If the salvage value on such property is more than 10 percent, you may disregard up to 10 percent of the salvage value in computing the cost basis on which you depreciate the asset.

The decline in value of the asset represents the *amount* you will be able to deduct on your tax return. The useful lifetime of the asset represents the *number of years* over which the deductions must be taken. To some extent, you can estimate the useful lifetime of your asset to further your own tax interests—shortening it if you wish quick deductions, lengthening it if deductions against high tax brackets in later years will produce greater tax savings.

Using Treasury Guidelines

The Treasury Department guidelines (discussed in the section on investment credits above) need not be followed exactly. But they give a good idea of the useful lifetimes which the Treasury considers "realistic."

If your own expectations differ from the average in the use of any business property, you may make your own estimate of its useful life and depreciate it on that basis. In estimating useful life you are expected to consider your experiences with similar equipment, how often you use it, your maintenance and repair policy, special weather conditions which may affect its performance, and similar factors. You will have no problems getting the I.R.S. to accept estimates falling within its depreciation guidelines. However, when the amounts involved are substantial, you may have to submit evidence to support estimates that fall outside normal limits.

A Controversy-Free Method

A simpler way of reaching an agreement with the I.R.S. over the expected useful life of your property entails the "Class Life System." It enables you to lump your purchases and give them a blanket treatment. You must use the Treasury's Asset Depreciation Range, but you may choose a "useful life" for each group of assets between the lower and upper limits permitted.

You may elect the Class Life method for any tax year. You do so by filing Form 4832 together with your tax return for the year in question. You must include all eligible property you have placed into service during the year. Each year, you must also file a report showing any changes in the account—property sold, etc.—which would affect your depreciation deduction. For tax purposes, you treat all assets in the account as part of the whole and ordinarily do not claim a gain or loss on sale or disposal of any individual item until the account is closed out.

With the Class Life system, you must compute depreciation on the straight line, declining balance, or sum of the years-digits methods. These are the methods most commonly used by business owners. Other methods which are allowed when regular depreciation procedures are followed—such as one which permits twice the straight line rate under certain circumstances—may not be used. Once you set up a Class Life account for a year's property acquisitions—a "vintage year"—you may make limited changes in your use of methods. But once you begin depreciating by the straight line method, you must adhere to it.

Note that when you elect to use the Class Life system for a tax year, you must include all eligible property placed into service during that year. If you wish, you may disregard the Class Life system in setting up depreciation formulas in succeeding years.

What happens if property is fully depreciated down to its salvage value but still has plenty of useful life? Of course, you are no longer entitled to depreciation deductions. If you sell the item for more than the stated salvage value you have estimated for it, you report the excess received as income. In effect, this is money you have already deducted on your tax return.

Pros, Cons of Rapid Depreciation

Estimating how long your business property will last is just that—a guess. While you are guessing, you might as well guess in the direction that does you the most good. The I.R.S. stresses, however, that estimates must be "reasonable."

It may often be unwise to assign too short a life to your depreciable assets. If you choose a depreciation period of less than three years for any property, it becomes ineligible for investment credits which may put more tax dollars back into your pockets than speeded-up deductions for depreciation could do. As noted on the preceding pages, only one-third of the investment in qualifying property with a useful life of at least three but less than five years is subject to the credit. Two-thirds of the amount invested is subject to the credit if the property has a useful life of at least five but less than seven years. Property must have a useful life of seven years or more to qualify for the full credit.

For most business owners, the Class Life system offers the best tax-saving possibilities. However, to employ it means in some cases that you must forgo other devices which could cut your tax bill. Before committing yourself to this system, it is advisable to figure whether using standard depreciation methods might do better for you in a given year.

TAX TREATMENT OF FRINGE BENEFITS

As we have previously discussed, there is a wide range of benefits your corporation can give your employees on a tax-free basis. You deduct the cost as a business expense and your employees need not report their value as income on their tax returns. When you have your own corporation and theoretically are its employee, you take tax-free benefits as an individual yet have your firm deduct the cost on its own return.

Payments you make for employees' group hospitalization and medical insurance are deductible as a business expense. Payments on employee group-term life insurance policies ordinarily are also deductible IF:

• The employees designate their own beneficiaries—and it is someone other than you.

• You retain *no* "incidents of ownership" over the policy.

You may insure your employees up to any amount and deduct the premiums. But if the amount of the policy exceeds $50,000, the employee must include in his gross income the cost of the excess coverage.

To be tax-deductible, the insurance must be group-term. This is protection for a fixed period of time provided under a master policy or a group of individual term policies. You must include all employees in this benefit provided they meet certain reasonable and consistent standards—for example, after they are in your employ for three months. Coverage must be made available to all employees according to the same ground rules.

Tax Treatment for Ordinary Life Policies

Ordinary life insurance policies—the "whole life" type written for a lifetime and not a specific term of years—take a different tax treatment. If a policy includes permanent insurance in which a cash value is built up, the policy must specify the portion of the premium allocated to the group-term feature. The employer may pay and deduct this portion, and the employee need not report it as income if the protection amounts to $50,000 or less. However, if the employer pays more than the amount needed to give the employee group-term coverage, the entire premium payment must be included in the employee's gross income and therefore becomes a taxable item.

In the uncommon cases where deductions for group-term life insurance premiums are disallowed, it is generally because the employer has limited coverage to certain employees—for example, those he likes.

To protect yourself against a successful I.R.S. challenge, you must put your group insurance plan in writing and let all employees know the basis upon which they will be covered. Make sure that if employees are to be excluded, it is for "reasonable and consistent standards." For instance, some firms include only their salaried workers—not members of unions which may have their own insurance programs.

Some group plans are held ineligible for deductions because they excessively favor stockholder-employees. Others have been challenged because they include independent contractors. As a rule, if you do not withhold income taxes or make Social Security contributions for persons doing work for you, they are not "employees" in the eyes of the law and not eligible for tax-free group insurance.

How "Split Dollar" Plans Work

"Split Dollar" life insurance plans also involve non-deductible premiums. They are so popular, however, because they theoretically provide instant benefits for employers at no overall cost. The typical "split dollar" policy on the life of an employee builds cash values over the years. At first it calls for the employee to pay that part of the premium which is allocated to pure term insurance. The employer pays the part of the premium which goes to build cash values. After a while dividends earned by the accumulated cash value are sufficient to cover the term insurance so that the employee's annual cost drops. The dividends may also be used to buy additional insurance that will pay the employer the full amount of his outlay. In this way the employee's beneficiaries get the full amount of the policy if he dies.

The employer retains rights to the cash value at all times. If the employee dies, the amount of the cash value is deducted from the face amount of the policy and reverts to the employer. Ultimately the employer gets back every dollar paid. Meanwhile, he has provided valuable insurance protection that should alleviate his employee's fears for his family's future and enable him to concentrate more fully on his job.

No Deductions for Beneficiary

It is a basic principle that an employer may not deduct premiums on an employee's life insurance policy if he is a beneficiary of the policy. The employer need not be named to receive the proceeds to be considered a beneficiary. He could benefit in indirect ways.

Say an employer takes an endowment insurance policy on the life of a valued employee. The latter names his own beneficiary. But the employer retains the right to cancel the policy and pocket its cash values if the employee quits or is fired. The employer still retains rights over the policy and therefore he may not deduct the premiums he pays.

Other Tax-Favored Benefits

Your corporation can give to employees—including yourself as its employee—other benefits that are tax-free to them while the corporation deducts the cost. Such benefits include:

• Discounts on goods and services. The value of discounts, enabling employees to obtain merchandise or services at prices lower than those charged the general public, is not generally included in their taxable income. The regulations say that to be tax-free, such discounts should be of "relatively small value," but the I.R.S. does not draw a clear line on this. Clothing shops, supermarkets, etc., give employees 20 percent or more off on all purchases without any backlash from the I.R.S. (Such discounts generally are not noted on the tax returns of either employer or employee.)

• Gifts on special occasions. At Christmas, for example, your corporation may give employees turkeys or other merchandise, and when the value is $25 or less they need not consider it as taxable income. The corporation may deduct the cost, however. (If it distributes cash, gift certificates, or other items readily convertible into cash, employees must consider their value as wages or salary.)

• Death benefits to the heirs of employees. Your firm may deduct such payments if the amount paid is "reasonable" in the light of the employee's service. The beneficiary need not include the first $5,000 of this compensation as income.

• Dues paid to professional or business clubs, chambers of commerce, trade associations, etc., which would be deductible by the employee if he paid them himself. Subscriptions to trade journals, etc., intended to help your employee do a better job, are also deductible when you pay them but are not considered as income to the employee.

• Educational expenses. You may set up an "educational assistance program" that pays the tuition of any courses your employees take. (Due to expire in 1983.)

• Convention trips. You may deduct the cost of attending meetings when the main purpose is to increase business knowledge or improve skills. When trips have a primary business purpose, the cost of transportation, food, lodging, etc. may be deducted.

• Ordinary moving expenses of employees—for example, when you relocate your headquarters. (You may deduct the amount you pay an employee because he has taken a loss on the sale of his old house, but the law says he must pay a tax on the amount received.)

• Meals and lodging furnished under certain circumstances. Your corporation may deduct the costs—and the employee need not report the value as income—when meals or lodging are furnished on its own premises for its own convenience, and the employee is required to accept the lodging as a condition of his employment. For example, a "live-in" servant, the employee of a summer resort subject to duty at odd hours, and a gas station attendant far from a populated area need not report the value of their lodging as wages.

Employees do not have to report the value of meals your corporation furnishes (although it may deduct the cost as a business expense) when the purpose is to keep them on hand for emergency calls during the meal period. The regulations say that such emergencies must either have occurred in the past or could reasonably be expected in the future.

In the same category are meals you furnish because the nature of your business restricts the employee to a meal period of 45 minutes or less and he cannot be expected to eat elsewhere in such a short time. (Say, if the nearest eating place is miles away.)

Reimbursement for Car Usage

Expenses involved in operating and maintaining an automobile to the extent that it is used in your trade or business are deductible, of course.

You are allowed to reimburse an employee for each mile he drives his car for business purposes. The employee must give an accounting to you, but he is not required to list the amount of his reimbursement on his own tax return. If an employee drives a car which gives high mileage per gallon and uses it a great deal for business, he can often make a tax-free profit with this arrangement. When you are technically your corporation's employee, you too may take a mileage allowance.

Almost everyone who uses a car for business is reimbursed on a mileage basis. It is also possible to deduct the actual cost of running the car on a percentage basis. To do this, add all car costs for the year—for depreciation, insurance, garage or other storage, gas, oil, check-ups, etc.—and then take the percentage of the total that is represented by business mileage. When an expensive car which gives comparatively low mileage per gallon is used, and when there is a high proportion of business use relative to personal use, this method may produce a higher tax deduction.

Why It Is Better for Employer to Pay

In many cases, the amount your corporation lays out on your or another employee's behalf would be deductible by him if he paid them himself. On the surface, there seems to be no overall tax saving when you make the payment.

In fact, however, the value of the deduction is generally greater to the employer than to the employee because the former is usually in a higher tax bracket. Say your employee pays $100 in hospital insurance premiums and can take a 25 percent deduction. His deduction is worth only $25 and he is still $75 out-of-pocket. If the corporation pays, your employee saves the entire $100. In that case, of course the corporation is out of pocket the $100 less the deduction which depends on its tax bracket.

Another tax-saving factor works for the employee when the employer makes payments for these fringe benefits directly, instead of adding the amount of such payments to salary. In order for the employee to get the deduction, he must file an itemized tax return. There may be no point in his doing this if his itemized deductions do not save the tax he may save by taking the standard deduction. When the employer pays and takes all the deductions himself, the employee gets the full value of the fringe. Even if his itemized deductions would amount to zero, he is still entitled to the standard deduction on his return.

This point has a special value for you as the owner of a closely-held corporation. You may give yourself all of these benefits as an employee, your corporation deducts for all of them, and you may still take the standard deduction.

WHEN YOUR CORPORATION RENTS SPACE

You may deduct as business expenses any rent you pay for property used for your business activities. This seems cut-and-dried and most owners of corporations have no trouble with it. They deduct rent paid or accrued on their tax returns, and never hear from the I.R.S. about the matter.

Once you get away from the simple matter of renting from an unrelated landlord, using the property exclusively for business purposes and paying your rent a month at a time, you may come up against special regulations.

These are some points to remember:

• Rent payments, to be deductible, must cover only the period for which the tax return is made. Say a business owner signed a lease in October, occupied the premises at once and paid a year's rent in advance. He may deduct only one-quarter of his payment on his return for the year. The rest of the payment—covering nine months in the following year—may be deducted only on his next year's return. This principle applies regardless of your method of accounting—whether you report income and outgo on a cash or accrual basis.

• Any repairs to maintain the property in an ordinary efficient operating condition are deductible at the time you pay for them—if you report on a cash basis—or at the time you contract for them if you report on an accrual basis.

There is a major distinction between "repairs" and "improvements." Work which brings plant, facilities or equipment back to a previous standard of appearance or performance is a "repair." Work which makes the value of property greater than it was before or extends its life well beyond normal expectations is usually considered an "improvement."

Repairs for which you will be allowed a full current deduction as a business expense include painting a building inside or out, pointing up the joints in brickwork, plastering cracks in walls and ceilings, repairing plumbing leaks, replacing missing roof shingles, and similar work to stop deterioration. Examples of work cited by the I.R.S. for which full current deductions may not be taken include a new roof, substantial lighting improvements (such as installation of a new wiring system or more modern fixtures), rebuilding a wall, and installing new plumbing fixtures.

When you make "improvements" to business property you occupy as a tenant, you may deduct an equal amount each year over the lifetime of your lease so that you will have taken a full deduction by the time your lease expires. (Under certain circumstances, when the improvements are made near the end of an existing lease and you have an option to renew, you will have to allocate the cost of the work over the number of years covered by your present and renewed lease.)

• If you make "repairs" and "improvements" at the same time, have your contractor or contractors give you separate bills for the different classes of work done. I.R.S. agents tend to think of small jobs as repairs and large ones as improvements, and tend not to question deductions for many small jobs made in one year when they might otherwise require deductions for one large job to be spread out over many years. The I.R.S. also says that if you fail to distinguish repairs from improvements, you may be required to capitalize the entire amount even though some of it might have been deducted at once as a business expense.

• If you rent from a family member or business associate, the I.R.S. says that to be deductible the payments must not be excessive. When you rent from a landlord who is unrelated to you, the I.R.S. probably will not question any but the most outlandish rent payments. Ordinarily, it will allow deductions that result from bad judgment on your part.

It is a different matter when the property is owned by someone related to you—your father or mother, husband or wife, son or daughter, say, or a business partner. The I.R.S. also looks closely at rental payments made by a corporation to a stockholder, the suspicion being that higher-than-usual rents are a device to take profits out of the corporation without paying a tax on them. The best defense against an I.R.S. challenge is the fact that the rents charged are no more than would be paid if the landlord were an outsider. If the I.R.S. finds evidence that the payment is excessive, it will reduce the deduction to cover the amount that would be paid in an arms-length transaction. Some tax experts believe the I.R.S. will not challenge deductions for rent 10 percent or so above the prevailing average.

• If you make improvements on property owned by a related taxpayer, you must deduct the cost of the improvement over the length of time it is expected to last, not how long your lease has to run.

The purpose of this regulation is to prevent one member of a family or business group from renting property from another, fixing it up and deducting the entire cost, then turning the improved property back to the landlord.

The I.R.S. defines a related taxpayer as a husband or wife, parents, grandparents, children, grandchildren, etc., but not a brother or sister. "Related persons" would also be an individual and a corporation of which 50 percent or more in value of the outstanding stock is owned directly or indirectly by or for that individual. Affiliated corporations which could file a consolidated return if they so chose are also "related."

• Billboards, signs, etc., that ordinarily would be expected to last as long as you occupy your premises should be capitalized—their cost deducted over the length of time your lease has to run.

● Lease deposits you forfeit on property used in your trade or business are deductible as a business loss for the year in which the amounts are forfeited.

● If, under the terms of your lease, you are required to pay increased taxes imposed upon the building you occupy, the additional expense is considered as rent and is deductible. This principle also covers sums paid to get out of a lease before the termination date originally called for.

● Expenses involved in moving from one business location to another are generally fully deductible at the time you incur them.

● If you pay someone to search for a suitable business location for you, you must follow special rules. The I.R.S. says that "commissions, bonuses, fees or other expenses you pay to obtain possession of property to be used in your business under a lease agreement covering a period of more than one year must generally be capitalized." Regardless of your method of accounting, you are expected to deduct the cost on an equal basis per year over the period of time the lease has to run.

ANGLES IN LEASING EQUIPMENT

Leasing of equipment of all kinds for business use has come on big in all fields in recent years. Sales representatives of equipment manufacturers list so many advantages for leasing that it sometimes seems that paying outright for what you want is out of style. In some cases, leasing is the best way of getting the things you need. But it also has many disadvantages which may make it completely inadvisable.

The major plus of leasing is that it does not require a large cash outlay for the purchase price at once. In a "buy now, pay later" environment, it seems easier to make 36 payments of $110 a month than one flat payment, of, say, $3,000. But the first point to remember is that on a dollar-and-cents basis, leasing almost always is more costly than an outright purchase. In effect, you are borrowing from the lessor to pay for the equipment. Hence a substantial interest charge is figured into the leasing rate. While "free" service is often provided with leased equipment, its cost—plus profit—is also figured in. You also pay a large sum to cover the depreciation of the equipment while it's in your hands. As a result of these factors, leasing usually does not offer a cost saving. Its main advantage is that it enables your corporation to conserve working capital. High cost is its main disadvantage.

Here is what leasing can do for you:

• You can take a full tax deduction against current income for the amount you pay out each month. In contrast, when you buy outright you are entitled only to a 10 percent investment credit applicable on depreciable business assets and a tax reduction based on depreciation of the property acquired. Most pieces of office furniture, fixtures, machines and equipment have a depreciation range of from 8 to 12 years.

• You minimize your immediate cash outlay. If the equipment produces income or saves expenses for you, its earning power may provide you with the money to pay its monthly cost to some extent.

• You are generally assured of good service on the equipment. The lessors have a stake in maintaining its good condition, so as to increase its ultimate retail value if it must later be sold. You can withhold payments if the promised service is not forthcoming and thus have a wedge to use in bargaining.

• Leasing preserves credit capacity. If you borrow from a bank to buy equipment, the amount is deducted from whatever maximum amount the bank thinks it safe to lend you. It may not consider a lease obligation in the same light and may keep your borrowing capacity undisturbed.

• If your credit lines are already extended, it is generally easier to lease equipment than to borrow the money to buy it. Leasing companies retain title to the equipment and need not worry about other creditors grabbing it as payment for your debts to them.

• Insurance considerations often cause an equipment user to opt for leasing. One reason for the boom in automobile leasing is that motorists who find it difficult or impossible—or financially prohibitive—to get individual insurance policies because of accident records or other factors, often can lease insured cars without trouble because the leasing firms hold huge umbrella policies.

Factors to Help You Decide

All factors considered, leasing is probably worth considering when two or more of these factors exist:

• When your corporation is low on cash and would have to borrow the money to pay for the equipment anyway.

● When it is at or near the limit of its ability to borrow from a bank, and you want to keep a certain amount of borrowing ability in reserve.

● When it is in the highest corporate tax bracket, and thus able to get the greatest benefit from deducting its leasing payments.

● When the equipment has a high rate of actual or potential obsolescence. By leasing, you avoid the likelihood that you will be the owner of suddenly outmoded items with a sharply reduced value. However, lessors of such equipment often charge higher rates during the early period of the lease to protect themselves against the obsolescence hazard.

● When you can put your money to work elsewhere where it will give you a higher return than you pay as a result of leasing.

● When there is a strong possibility that changing circumstances will make it desirable for you to shift to other equipment AND your leasing contract enables you to discontinue present arrangements without excessive penalty.

On the other hand, not much can be gained from leasing if:

● You have enough cash to pay for the equipment outright.

● You are getting less interest on your cash than the interest charges you would have to pay when you lease.

● The equipment has a long life and you are likely to keep it until it is pretty much worn out.

● You are now in a relatively low tax bracket and would not gain substantially from a deduction for the leasing payments. OR you are likely to be in a higher bracket in later years, when deductions for depreciation will keep more money in your pocket.

Lots of Pencil Work Needed

You may face lots of work with pencil and paper before determining whether it is better to buy or lease. To arrive at the real costs of buying, you have to put down the actual sales price, what that money will earn for you over the time span you are comparing, what you estimate it will cost to service the equipment for that period, and what your insurance costs will be. Add these figures and subtract the estimated value of the equipment at the end of the period under consideration. Next make allowance for tax factors. Subtract the taxes on what your money would earn. Also subtract the actual tax reduction you obtain from depreciation and from your insurance payments. What you now have is your actual dollar cost of buying the item in question.

To get a realistic picture of leasing costs, add your monthly payments for the period, plus service costs if any. Add any insurance costs that you must pay directly. Subtract your tax saving. Say your corporation is in the 48 percent tax bracket and you pay $6,000 for three years. Your tax saving is $2,880. Next subtract whatever extra value you might get by exercising the option to buy the equipment at the end of the leasing period. If you can buy it for $400 and sell it for $600, you have a $200 asset (less any applicable taxes). You now have a bottom line figure to compare with the comparable figure showing the actual cost of a purchase.

As the foregoing indicates, the question can become quite complicated. But you can take the word of experts who have slide-ruled the question that leasing generally is more expensive than its alternatives. Experts say that if you decide to lease on the basis of non-cost factors, it is up to you to prove your choice is wise.

CHARITY AND YOUR CORPORATION

A corporation may deduct contributions totaling no more than 5 percent of its taxable income. If contributions in any year exceed the 5 percent limitation, the corporation may carry over the excess and take credit for it in each of five succeeding years. Say you give $10,000 of your corporate income to charity this year and your taxable income for the year totals only $100,000. You take a deduction for $5,000 this year, and a deduction for the rest in the next five years, as long as your total charitable deductions in those years do not exceed the 5 percent limitation. But you may not deduct for a carried-over contribution if it increases net operating loss carryover.

If you have a corporation, consider whether you can gain a greater deduction by making contributions personally or through your firm. The taxpayer with the higher tax rate is, of course, the better choice to make them. If you take the standard 15 percent deduction on your personal return, you may not deduct separately for contributions. Hence, as we have noted, it is better to contribute through your corporation.

Although you ordinarily may not deduct the value of time spent working for a charity, your corporation could pay full salaries to you and/or your employees when they devote some of their time to such causes. These payments are generally tax-deductible to the corporation. A Treasury spokesman says wages or salaries paid for a "modest amount" of charitable activity during working hours usually will not be questioned. The I.R.S. allowed one company to deduct 20 percent of the salary it paid an executive while he did church missionary work in Asia.

Business owners are often asked to contribute stock in trade which charities then sell at bazaars, etc. At one time you could deduct the fair market value of contributed items, but the regulations now say you may deduct no more than their cost to you. Many merchants have outdated or damaged merchandise they could sell only at lower-than-cost prices. By giving it to charity, they may achieve better financial results than if they sold it outright and pocketed all the proceeds.

As a matter of policy, it is unwise to donate business property that has declined below your cost or other basis. You may deduct only the fair market value of the donated item. If you first sell the item, you may take a deduction for the amount you lost on the transaction plus a deduction for the full amount you then contribute to charity.

Say you bought a building ten years ago for $25,000. You have depreciated it so that your present cost basis stands at $16,000. But the building has become so run down that you can get only $10,000 for it. Sell it yourself, and you have a loss of $6,000 you can apply against other capital gains or income. If you are in a 40 percent tax bracket, that is a $2,400 tax saving. Give the proceeds of the sale to charity and in addition you get as much of a tax deduction as you would have received if you gave it the building in the first place.

DEDUCTING FOR CASUALTY LOSSES

The rules about deducting losses due to casualty or theft from the taxable income you report to the Internal Revenue Service seem simple enough: You may deduct the full amount of your business losses, and all but the first $100 in each case of personal loss.

When it comes to questions of what constitutes a deductible loss, how you establish the amount of your true loss, and how you prove your case to the Treasury department, the rules can become sticky and, in some cases, open to different interpretations.

To make your deductions for casualty losses stick if they are questioned by the I.R.S., you will have to provide information concerning:

- The exact nature of the casualty.
- Date it occurred.
- Your ownership of the property.
- Its cost to you, as proved by a sales contract or receipt, cancelled check used in payment, etc.
- What depreciation if any you have taken on the property.
- Values before and after the casualty.
- How much you got from the insurance company for the damage, and how much repair, restoration or cleanup work was done for you free by relief agencies.

In cases of theft, you must submit records concerning the above points except the date of occurrence. There is a distinction between "theft" and unexplained loss, however. You are expected to prove that there was an "unlawful taking and removing of your property with the intent to deprive you of it." Hence it is important to get on the record evidence of unlawfulness in the form of statements of witnesses, broken locks or windows, etc. The fact that you have provided the police with evidence of theft generally satisfies the I.R.S. on this point.

How Losses Are Established

Difficulties sometimes arise over what constitutes a casualty. According to the working definition, a casualty is the destruction in whole or in part of property as a result of a specific event occurring suddenly and without warning. Fitting this description are what are normally described as accidents—a car crash, for example—as well as damages from fire, flood or unexpected acts of vandalism. According to traditional interpretations by the Treasury Department, not fitting the definition is "progressive deterioration" of property over a period of time—the undermining of a building's foundations by ground settlement, for example. Nor can a casualty loss be claimed when property values drop as a result of nearby disasters. Owners of buildings unaffected by a California earthquake could not sustain claims of loss as a result of lowered property values in the region.

In recent years, tax courts have been more liberal in allowing deductions for casualty losses than has the I.R.S., however.

By definition, theft consists of the unlawful taking of property or money with the intention of keeping it permanently. The definition excludes property you may have lost, misplaced or otherwise cannot account for, as well as losses you may have incurred because property you bought was misrepresented to you or wore out sooner than you were told it would.

The key to making your deductions stick may lie in the way you prove the value of the items that have been damaged or stolen. Getting acceptable proof may be difficult in the case of used items. If the article has been stolen or destroyed and you have used it for business and have depreciated it, you can use its adjusted cost basis (original cost minus all depreciation taken on it) as its present value. If it has been only partially damaged, you must establish its value immediately before and immediately after the casualty. The value must be "objective"—what the property would be worth to a disinterested third party.

How "Market Value" Is Figured

"Fair market value" can usually be established to the Treasury's satisfaction in one of three ways:

• Appraisal. The word of a competent appraiser familiar with sales of similar property generally carries great weight. His report for your files should cite his background, his knowledge of current market conditions, and the methods he has used to determine the extent of your loss. It helps to have photos showing the amount of damage; from such photos the extent of work required to restore the property to its former condition can more easily be determined.

• Established guide books, such as the monthly price manuals issued by automobile organizations listing current prices for different makes and models.

• Actual repair or replacement cost. A contractor's itemized bill for repairs is usually acceptable if you also show that the repairs were needed to restore the property to its condition before the casualty, but have not made it better or more valuable than before. Another proviso is that the repair cost cannot be excessive—more than is generally charged for the work involved. A sales slip is acceptable if it shows that the item purchased merely duplicates destroyed or stolen property and does not cover something better or more valuable.

When to Take Deductions

You generally may deduct a casualty loss only in the year in which it happened, regardless of when repairs or replacement occurred. Losses due to theft or embezzlement, on the other hand, may be deducted only in the year in which they were discovered—not necessarily when they occurred.

Suppose your business car is demolished in an accident in late December. You carry no collision insurance but the other party in the accident seems clearly at fault and it is likely that you can recover the cost of the car. If you do not collect by the end of your tax year, the amount of the loss deducted on your return must be reduced by the amount you expect to get.

But say the next year you get less than you expected—and less than the depreciated value of the car. On your return for the year, you may deduct the amount that represents your actual loss.

Or suppose a court awards you a judgment of $4,000 to cover the exact amount of your loss. But it soon becomes evident that the person the judgment was entered against is unable to pay. You can claim your loss in that year in which you realize you have no chance of getting paid.

On the other hand, suppose you collect more than you expected, and more than the car's depreciated value. It is not necessary to go back and recompute your tax for the year in which you claimed a loss. But you must report the additional amount received as income for the year in which you received it.

Rules on "Involuntary Conversion"

"Involuntary conversion" is the term the I.R.S. uses to describe what happens when you are compensated by an insurance company or some one else for the damage or theft of your property. When this conversion occurs, it could produce a gain or loss. For tax purposes, you usually must report the gain or loss in the year in which it occurs. If the property has been held six months or less, the gain or loss is treated as ordinary income or loss. Gain or loss from a casualty or theft of property held longer than six months may be treated as a capital gain or loss, except if the property is part of your stock in trade or is held primarily for sale in the ordinary course of your business operations.

In cases when you receive replacement property similar or related in service or use to the original property involved in the casualty loss, the gain from the exchange is not taxed at once. Example: The state condemns for public use an undeveloped lot you use for parking by callers at your office. The lot has an adjusted cost basis of $5,000. The state offers you another lot across the street worth $7,500. Although you have a paper profit of $2,500 on the deal, you need not report it as income. When you sell the second lot, however, for tax purposes you figure its cost as the price you paid for the first lot less any deductions for depreciation.

In other casualty and theft cases, when you register a gain in money or unlike property, you need not report it as taxable income if you purchase replacement property costing as much or more than the original property. (You may also elect not to report the gain immediately if you acquire control of a corporation which owns such property.)

An I.R.S. example: A business building with an adjusted cost basis of $18,000 is destroyed by a hurricane. The owner receives $22,000 from an insurance company in the same year to compensate him for the damages. He puts up a new building at once at a cost of $19,000 and thus has $3,000 in cash left over. He has made a theoretical profit of $4,000 on the deal (he got $22,000 for a building presumably worth $18,000) but since $1,000 of that "windfall" was used for the replacement, he may elect not to report that amount as gain. But he must include the unspent balance of $3,000 in his gross income. If he had spent the $3,000 on the new building, he could have avoided reporting that amount as well, of course.

Certain requirements must be met for property to qualify as "replacement property" and thus to enable you to defer taxes on gains. It must serve a purpose similar to the property involved in the casualty loss. And it must be acquired within two years after the close of the first tax year in which you realized any part of the gain. (If you have a good reason for not making the replacement within the authorized time period, you may apply to the I.R.S. for an extension of the time period.)

In determining your gain or loss from a casualty or theft, any costs you incur in seeking compensation can be deducted from the amount received. These costs might include appraisers' fees, legal costs, costs of "before" and "after" photos, travel, and other expenses connected with your attempts to negotiate a settlement.

Appendix

A Glossary of Accounting and Legal Terms
Used in Establishing and Operating Corporations

ACCOUNTING PERIOD. A part of the business year at the conclusion of which time income and balance sheet statements are prepared. Some businesses use quarterly accounting periods, but many prepare balance sheets and income statements every six months. Annual statements are often audited by outside auditors.

ACCUMULATED SURPLUS. The surplus which an enterprise acquires as a result of profits and not the contribution of shareholders. Also known as earned surplus.

ARTICLES OF INCORPORATION. The form prepared by incorporators of a company containing details of its organization. It is necessary to submit this form to the designated official in order to be chartered to do business within the state.

ASSIGNMENT. Any bill of sale, deed, declaration of trust or other instrument which transfers ownership or control of shares of stock from one person to another.

AUTHORIZED STOCK. The total number of shares of stock a corporation is permitted to issue by its original or amended articles of incorporation. A corporation need not issue all of its authorized stock. Fees payable to the state are generally based on the total number of authorized shares, and therefore incorporators often keep the total number of authorized shares to the minimum provided by law.

BY-LAWS. The rules adopted by a corporation specifying the conditions under which it will be operated. Corporate by-laws must conform to the articles of incorporation filed with the state, and also with state laws concerning responsibilities, rights and duties of directors, officers and majority and minority shareholders.

CANCELLATION. To cancel a share means to eliminate it from the authorized shares of the corporation. In effect this reduces the total number of shares the corporation is then authorized to issue.

CAPITAL. Money or other assets of value which stockholders contribute to a business to enable it to operate. "Capital" of an established corporation generally consists of the contribution of the shareholders plus accumulated profits. It is the total worth of the business after all liabilities are deducted.

CAPITALIZATION. The total value of all securities of a business enterprise. Capitalization also includes long term debt and consists of what would have to be paid to investors and long term creditors if the business were liquidated.

CAPITAL STOCK. The total amount of stock a corporation is authorized to issue by its articles of incorporation. The total number of shares issued, and the value assigned to them, often do not indicate the amount of dollars actually involved. Stock may carry a low par value, or no par value at all, even though the true value per share is considerable. When the amount contributed in cash or property for each share of stock exceeds the par or stated value, the additional value is shown on the balance sheet as paid-in surplus.

CAPITAL SURPLUS. This includes any surplus of a corporation greater than the earned surplus arising out of the retention of profits. It may include the paid-in surplus—the true value of shares in the corporation over and above the stated value. It may also result from a revaluation of assets, including "good will."

CERTIFICATE OF INCORPORATION. This term is often used synonymously with Articles of Incorporation. It is also known as the corporation charter—the authorization by a state permitting a business firm to operate in its jurisdiction.

CLERK. Title of the person who, in some states, has the duties of a secretary. (See below.)

CLOSE OR CLOSED CORPORATION. One in which most or all of the stock is held by a small number of persons. Some states define a close corporation as one with fewer than twenty shareholders. A corporation which makes shares widely available to outsiders is known as a public or open corporation.

COMMON STOCK. This is corporate stock which usually gives each holder voting rights and entitles him to dividends if the corporation is profitable and does not need to retain all its earnings for its own purposes. Other kinds of stock are preferred stock, which usually promises its holders a stated dividend per year but perhaps no voting privileges, and convertible preferred stock, which carries the privileges of preferred stock and gives holders the right to convert their shares into common stock according to a specified formula. Some owners of corporations use common, preferred and convertible preferred stock to achieve specific estate-planning objectives.

CONSPICUOUS. When state law requires that a term, clause or notation in a message to shareholders must be "conspicuous," the word is generally defined as being presented in a way that a reasonable person against whom the clause is to operate can notice it. A "conspicuous" notation can be a heading—for example, IRREVOCABLE PROXY—printed in capitals. A message is considered "conspicuous" if it is set in type larger or in a different color from that in the body of the message. State laws usually declare that any term contained in a telegram is "conspicuous," as are words stamped or typewritten on a share certificate.

CORPORATION CALENDAR. A list of the duties which a corporation, officers and directors must perform during the year. Such a calendar is prepared to meet requirements of the certificate of incorporation—holding of annual meetings at the prescribed time, for example—and to remind corporate officers of deadlines by which they must file reports to stockholders and federal, state and possibly local governments.

DOMESTIC CORPORATION . One incorporated in the state in which its headquarters are located. When it establishes branches or offices in other states, it is regarded there as a "foreign" corporation.

DOMICILE. The state in which a company is organized and from which it receives its authorization to do business. Many corporations are domiciled in states other than those in which they conduct most of their activities. More than a third of all corporations listed on the New York and American Stock Exchanges are domiciled in Delaware, but only a small fraction of them conduct their main activities in that state.

DOUBLE TAXATION. A term used to describe a two-time levy upon income or wealth. Income earned by a corporation is often doubly taxed. The corporation first pays a tax on its profits, and its shareholders are then taxed on profits it distributes in the form of dividends.

DUMMY. A term used to describe the first directors of a newly-formed corporation who sit only until other directors are elected by the shareholders.

EARNED SURPLUS. That part of the surplus of a corporation which represents profits it has retained since its organization. In complicated corporate structures, earned surplus may also include portions of surpluses developed by other firms that have subsequently been merged, consolidated or acquired. Earned surplus may also go under the label of retained earnings or retained income.

EMPLOYEE. In the present context, employees are all persons on the regular corporate payroll. A person who owns all the stock of a corporation but also takes a salary for regular services is an employee.

EQUITY. The net investment which shareholders have in their business. Equity is another term for net worth—which is left for the owners after all liabilities are deducted from assets.

FIDUCIARY. An executor, administrator, trustee, guardian, receiver, trustee in bankruptcy, assignee for the benefit of creditors, committee, conservator, curator, custodian, partner, agent, officer of a corporation public or private, public officer, nominee or any other person acting in money matters for a person, trust or estate. A fiduciary may also be "anyone who holds something in trust for another." State laws hold anyone in a fiduciary capacity to strict standards of conduct.

FINANCIAL STATEMENT. A compilation of assets and liabilities. It is usually prepared at least once a year for business organizations, at the end of a fiscal period. It may be shown to the state, stockholders, creditors or others. "Financial statement" and "balance sheet" are usually synonymous for corporations.

FOREIGN CORPORATION. One operating in a state different from that in which it was originally chartered. A corporation may have all its offices and conduct all its activities in one state, yet be considered "foreign" there because it has received its original certificate of incorporation from a different state.

"GOOD ACCOUNTING PRACTICES." Such practices must be observed by corporations whenever the interests of minority shareholders are involved. In this context, "good accounting practices" usually are the standard procedures recommended by the American Institute of Certified Public Accountants and similar bodies recognized as reputable by the accounting profession.

"GOOD FAITH." As applied to an officer or director, it means total honesty in the conduct of the corporate business, putting the corporation's interests above those of the individual. It also means that a reasonable effort will be made to ascertain all facts of a question before a judgment is made on the corporation's behalf.

INCOME STATEMENT. A summary of income and expenses of a business over a specified period of time, with the "bottom line" showing a profit or loss. Also known as profit and loss statement, earning statement, operating statement, etc., an income statement may be issued in connection with a balance sheet or financial statement.

INCORPORATOR. A person who signs the articles of incorporation which an enterprise files with state authorities when it seeks approval to operate as a corporation.

INITIAL CAPITAL. A term sometimes used in financial statements to indicate the surplus held by a firm at the beginning of the reporting period covered by the statement. The amount existing at the end of the period will represent additions or subtractions in the form of profits retained, or losses or dividends paid, during the period.

INSIDE DIRECTOR One who is also an officer, employee or significant stockholder. An inside director generally represents "management," while an outside director—neither an employee nor major stockholder—generally takes a more objective viewpoint. Many firms have more outside than inside directors.

INSOLVENCY. The inability to pay debts as they become due in the usual course of business.

INTERLOCKING DIRECTOR. A director of two or more corporations allied to each other in some visible way—for example, owning some of each other's shares or controlled by the same stockholders. It is usually illegal for one person to hold directorships in corporations which are competitive.

IN WRITING. In legal terminology, "in writing" and "written" include any way of putting words on paper. Texts such as bylaws or articles of incorporation must be "in writing" but they can be printed, typewritten, mimeographed, or put on paper in any other readable form. Signatures "in writing" may be individually placed on paper by the signatory, but facsimile signatures may be placed on corporate bonds, stock certificates, etc.

ISSUED STOCK. Shares which have been distributed to shareholders or issued and held in the treasury. Issued stock is also known as outstanding stock.

LIMITED LIABILITY. A phrase describing the fact that shareholders of a corporation generally have no personal responsibility for its debts and cannot be assessed for its liabilities beyond the amount they have contributed. Thus a shareholder can ordinarily lose no more than what he has paid for his stock. Under some circumstances, however, shareholders may be held responsible for wages due employees of a bankrupt company.

MANAGEMENT STOCK. Stock held by persons actively engaged in the operation of a corporation. The term is also used to describe shares issued to directors or officers to assure them that they will have control of the company even though holders of other classes of stock may have a greater financial stake in it.

NET ASSETS. The amount by which total assets of a corporation exceed its total debts.

NON-ASSESSABLE STOCK. Stock which owners have fully paid for and which entails no further liabilities regardless of the financial difficulties the corporation may get into. Stock certificates generally carry the words "fully paid and non-assessable" to indicate that shareholders cannot be held responsible for obligations the corporation itself cannot meet.

NO PAR VALUE STOCK. Stock with no stated value, generally issued to reduce the fee payable when a corporation is formed or a new stock issue is approved. States usually tax issued stock according to its stated value—the higher the par value, the higher the tax. For other purposes, common stock without par value usually is worth just as much as stock that carries a stated value. The true measurement of value is what a share will bring in the market.

OPEN CORPORATION. One with stock the general public can buy easily. Like its "closed" counterpart, an open corporation may have one shareholder or a group of shareholders who own more than 50 percent of the shares and hence can dictate corporate policy.

OPERATING SURPLUS. The amount remaining at the end of a corporation's reporting period after expenses, taxes, and dividends are deducted. It represents total earnings after taxes, less any amount that may have been distributed to shareholders. At the end of the fiscal period, operating surplus is added on the books to earned surplus which consists of all retained profits.

OUTSTANDING STOCK. All the shares held by individual shareholders. Together with treasury stock—shares formerly issued but later bought back or redeemed by the company—outstanding stock equals issued stock.

PAID-UP CAPITAL. The total amount paid by shareholders for their shares of capital stock. On a balance sheet, paid-up capital represents the total stated value (par or no-par) of common stock plus what shareholders have paid in excess of the stated value.

PAID-IN SURPLUS. The surplus created when shareholders pay more for their stock than the stated value per share. It represents the difference between the paid-up capital and the stated value (par or no par) of the corporate shares.

PARTICIPATING STOCK. A type of preferred stock which entitles holders to additional dividends when profits exceed a certain amount. Participating stock usually is entitled to a fixed amount in dividends per year. If specified dividends are paid on common stock, the participating and common shareholders may receive additional dividends. Owners of small corporations often issue participating stock to prospective heirs, enabling the latter to share in the profits of a corporation but without voting privileges. In this way control of the firm may remain in the hands of a few persons who hold the common stock with voting privileges.

PERSON. In legal usage, any legal or commercial entity—an individual, corporation, trust, estate, partnership or association, two or more persons sharing a joint or common interest, etc.

PERSONAL SERVICE CORPORATION. See professional corporation below.

PREEMPTIVE RIGHTS. Rights giving shareholders the opportunity to buy their proportionate amount of any new stock offerings made by the corporation. These rights can be limited or denied in the articles of incorporation. Many states specify that unless its articles of incorporation provide otherwise, a corporation may sell shares to employees without offering them to shareholders first. Terms and conditions of such sales usually must be approved by the holders of two-thirds of the existing shares, so that in effect the shareholders retain control over how additional shares will be issued or sold.

PREFERRED STOCK. Stock with preferential features over other stock of the same corporation. Typically, preferred stock is entitled to dividends of a specified amount each year, and these must be paid before less preferred or common shares receive any dividends at all. Preferred stock often carries no voting privileges, except when the corporation defers dividends for a specified period of time. If dividends on preferred stock go unpaid, they usually then accumulate, adding to the debt of the corporation.

PRIOR PREFERENCE STOCK. Preferred stock with superior rights to dividends before other preferred stock.

PROFESSIONAL CORPORATION. Also known as a personal service corporation, this is one organized for the specific purpose of rendering a professional service. In most states, a professional corporation must have as its shareholders only individuals who are licensed or otherwise legally authorized to render the particular service. Professional corporations also differ from commercial corporations in that their income is derived primarily from work performed by the owners, rather than from the use of invested capital. Practitioners of professional services who have incorporated include public accountants, chiropractors, dentists, osteopaths, physicians and surgeons, podiatrists, chiropodists, architects, engineers, veterinarians, attorneys at law and life insurance agents.

PRO FORMA. A latin phrase meaning "a matter of form." A pro forma balance sheet is not a true one of an operating corporation, but may be one showing the assets and liabilities of an enterprise if it were established. A pro forma financial statement is often issued when corporations consider merging. The statement shows what the present financial picture would be like if the companies had merged at an earlier time.

PROSPECTUS. A document issued with the intention of interesting potential investors or lenders. A typical prospectus for a corporation describes its business, prospects and problems, and gives an appraisal of its profit potentialities. It generally includes a pro forma financial statement (see above) and other data which a reasonably intelligent investor of average prudence should have to make a sound investment decision.

REDEEMABLE STOCK. Stock which can be bought back by the issuing corporation at a date and price specified at the time it is issued. It is usually preferred stock. Corporations sometimes issue such stock when capital is needed and redeem it after the firm becomes profitable. When preferred stock is redeemed, more of the corporation's after-tax profits can be distributed as dividends to common shareholders.

RETIREMENT. To "retire" a share means to restore it to the status of an authorized but unissued share.

SEAL. An impression of a design made by a press upon paper. A corporate seal does not require ink and has no adhesive substance. Some states require or permit the seal of a corporation to be placed upon a certificate of stock, corporate bond or other corporate document. The "seal" might also be a facsimilie, engraved or printed.

SECRETARY. The officer of a corporation whose duties are often prescribed by the laws of the state and by the articles of incorporation or bylaws. The secretary usually is responsible for making and keeping records of all proceedings and transactions at meetings of directors or shareholders, the issuing of corporate notices of annual or special meetings, and the maintaining of corporate records. A secretary in some states is described as a clerk.

SECURITY. Any share of stock, bond, debenture, note or other security issued by a corporation and registered as to ownership on the books of the corporation.

SHARES. The units into which the ownership interests in a corporation are divided.

SHAREHOLDER. A holder of record of shares in a corporation. For ownership purposes, a shareholder becomes an owner as soon as he purchases or otherwise acquires shares. However, he usually is not entitled to vote until he is registered on the books of the corporation.

STATED CAPITAL. The sum of the par value of all issued shares of the corporation having a par value; and other amounts that have been transferred to the stated capital of the corporation.

STOCK RECORD DATE. The date established by a corporation to be used in determining stock ownership for dividend purposes. Ownership of shares may be transferred for some time, perhaps two or three weeks, before the record of the transfer is actually made. It is possible that one who has recently sold stock in a corporation may still be recorded as its owner and receive a dividend that has been declared. A shareholder who sells stock before the record date and who subsequently receives a dividend from it, is required to turn it over to the buyer.

STOCK REGISTER. The record of stock ownership kept by the registrar of a corporation to designate the owner of record of shares at any given time.

SUBSCRIBED CAPITAL. The amount of money promised by prospective shareholders of a business, generally one just getting started. Subscribed capital becomes paid-in capital when shareholders pay for stock they have promised to buy.

SUBSCRIBER. One who makes a commitment to purchase shares in a corporation.

SUBSIDIARY. One company which is controlled by another through ownership of all or most of its stock.

SURPLUS. The amount by which net assets of a corporation exceed its stated capital.

TRANSFER. A change on the books of a corporation in the registered ownership of a security.

TRANSFER AGENT. A person or concern which transfers stock ownership from one person to another and handles the details of destroying old shares and issuing new ones in the name of the new owner. Small firms generally serve as their own transfer agent. Publicly-held corporations usually employ a bank, trust company, or similar organization.

TRANSFER BOOK. The volume in which are recorded the names of all registered owners of corporate stock with the number of shares owned by each person. The transfer book is the source of the list to which notices of meetings of stockholders are mailed and dividends paid.

TOTAL SURPLUS. Often used in balance sheets, this term represents the sum of all surpluses—earned and capital surplus and additions to surplus.

TREASURY SHARES. Shares which were issued but subsequently acquired by the corporation and neither cancelled nor retired after their acquisition. Such shares often are held for possible future sale to the public, for distribution to shareholders as dividends, or for sale to employees under stock option plans. Treasury shares are included in the total number of shares issued but are not considered outstanding for dividend, quorum, voting or other purposes.

VOTES. As used with respect to actions of shareholders, this term includes votes as the term is commonly understood as well as waivers, releases, consents, writings signed by shareholders instead of taking action at a meeting of shareholders, and all objections or dissents made by shareholders in conformance with state laws.

By-Laws That May Be Adapted or Used As Is By Small Business and Professional Corporations

The by-laws below will serve the needs of most small corporations. They may be adapted to fit particular circumstances. In general, it is best to keep by-laws as simple as state law permits and free of restrictions that will hamper you in operating your corporation.

* * *

BY-LAWS
of

ARTICLE I – OFFICES

1. PRINCIPAL OFFICE. The principal office of the corporation shall be established and maintained in the (city, town, village) of _____ , County of _____ , State of _____ .

2. OTHER OFFICES. The corporation may have other offices at other places and in any state which the board of directors ("the board") may establish from time to time.

ARTICLE II – SHAREHOLDERS

1. PLACE AND TIME OF MEETINGS. Upon due notice, regular and special meetings of shareholders shall be held at the principal office of the corporation or at such other place as the board shall authorize. The annual meeting of shareholders shall be held on the _____ day in the month of ____ _____ in each year, at the hour of _____o'clock____M., or at such other time as the board shall fix, in order to elect directors and to transact other business that may come before the meeting. If the date set for the annual meeting is a legal holiday, the meeting shall be held on the next business day. If the election of directors is not held on the designated day, the election shall be held at a meeting of shareholders as soon thereafter as is convenient.

2. SPECIAL MEETINGS. Meetings of shareholders may be called for any purpose by the president upon the request of the holders of 10 percent or more of all outstanding shares of the corporation entitled to vote at the meeting.

3. NOTICE OF MEETINGS. Written notice stating where and when the meeting will be held and, in case of a special meeting, its purpose, shall be delivered not less than ten nor more than fifty days before the date of the meeting to each shareholder of record entitled to vote at the meeting. Delivery shall be made personally or by mail. If mailed, such notice shall be deemed to be delivered when deposited with full postage in an official U.S. mail depository and addressed to the shareholder at his address as it appears on the stock transfer books of the corporation.

4. CLOSING OF TRANSFER BOOKS OR FIXING OF RECORD DATE. In order to determine which shareholders are entitled to notice of or to vote at any meeting or adjournment thereof, or which shareholders are entitled to receive payment of any dividend, or to make a listing of shareholders for any other purpose, the board may provide that the stock transfer books be closed for a period not to exceed fifty days. Such books shall be closed for at least ten days immediately before such meeting.

5. RECORD OF SHAREHOLDERS. The officer or agent in charge of the stock transfer books shall make a complete record of the shareholders entitled to vote at each meeting or any adjournment of such meeting. The list shall be in alphabetical order and shall contain the address of and number of shares held by each shareholder. The list shall be produced at the meeting and may be inspected by any shareholder during the meeting.

6. PROXIES. At any meeting of shareholders, a shareholder may vote in person or may be represented by a proxy executed by the shareholder or by his or her authorized attorney-in-fact. Such proxy shall be filed with the secretary of the corporation before the meeting is called to order.

7. QUORUM. A majority of the outstanding shares entitled to vote shall constitute a quorum at such meetings. If less than a majority of the outstanding shares are represented, a majority of the shares represented may adjourn the meeting without further notice. At an adjourned meeting at which a quorum shall be represented in person or by proxy, any business may be transacted which could have been appropriately transacted at the original meeting. Shareholders represented at a duly organized meeting may continue to transact business until the meeting is adjourned, even if withdrawals of shareholders result in the presence of less than a quorum.

8. VOTING OF SHARES. At any regular or special meeting of shareholders, each outstanding share entitled to vote shall be entitled to one vote upon each matter submitted to a vote.

9. VOTING OF SHARES UNDER CERTAIN CIRCUMSTANCES. Shares held by an administrator, executor or guardian may be voted by him in person or by proxy, and it shall not be required that such shares be transferred into his name. Shares held in the name of a trustee may be voted by him in person or by proxy, but a trustee shall not be entitled to vote shares held by him unless and until such shares are transferred into his name.

Shares held by, in the name of, or under the control of a receiver may be voted by him, and it shall not be required that shares be transferred into his name if he has been empowered to vote such shares by order of the court by which he was appointed.

Treasury shares of its own stock held by the corporation shall not be voted at any meeting or counted in determining the total number of shares outstanding for purposes of any meeting.

10. ACTION BY SHAREHOLDERS WITHOUT A MEETING. Any action required or permitted to be taken at a meeting of the shareholders may be taken without a meeting if a consent in writing, agreeing to the proposed action, shall be signed by all of the shareholders entitled to vote upon the subject matter.

11. CUMULATIVE VOTING. At each election for directors, every shareholder entitled to vote shall have the right to vote, in person or by proxy, the number of shares owned by him for as many persons as there are directors to be elected. He shall also be entitled, if he so desires, to cumulate his votes by giving one candidate as many votes as the number of such directors multiplied by the number of his shares shall equal, or by distributing such votes among any number of such candidates.

ARTICLE III – BOARD OF DIRECTORS

1. GENERAL POWERS. The business and affairs of the corporation shall be managed by its board of directors.

2. NUMBER AND TENURE OF DIRECTORS. The number of directors of the corporation shall be _____ . Each director shall hold office until the next annual meeting of shareholders and until his successor has been elected and qualified.

3. REGULAR MEETINGS. A regular meeting of the board shall be held without other notice immediately after, and at the same place as, the annual meeting of shareholders. The board may resolve to hold other regular meetings without notice.

4. SPECIAL MEETINGS. Special meetings of the board may be called by or at the request of the president or any ____ directors. The person or persons authorized to call such special meetings may determine where they shall be held.

5. NOTICE OF MEETING. Notice of a special meeting shall be given at least two days previously by notice delivered personally, mailed to each director at his given address, or delivered by telegram. Any director may waive notice of any meeting. Attendance of a director at a meeting shall constitute a waiver of notice of the meeting, except when a director attends a meeting in order to object to the transaction of any business because the meeting has not been lawfully called or convened.

6. QUORUM. A majority of the authorized number of directors shall constitute a quorum for the transaction of business at any meeting of the board. If less than a majority is present at a meeting, a majority of the directors present may adjourn the meeting without further notice.

7. MANNER OF ACTING. When a majority of the directors act at a meeting at which a quorum is present, their action will be recognized as the action of the board.

8. ACTION WITHOUT A MEETING. An action by the board of directors

may be taken without a meeting if a consent in writing, agreeing to the action so taken, shall be signed by all of its directors.

9. FILLING OF VACANCIES. A vacancy occurring in the board of directors may be filled by a vote of a majority of the directors remaining, even though they represent less than a quorum. A director elected to fill such vacancy shall be elected for the unexpired term in office of his predecessor.

10. COMPENSATION. If so voted by the board, each director may be paid expenses of attending each meeting of the board. He may also be paid a stated salary as director, a fixed sum for attending each meeting of the board, or both.

11. PRESUMPTION OF AGREEMENT. A director who is present at a meeting at which action is taken on a corporate matter shall be presumed to have agreed to the decision reached unless he shall request that his dissent be entered in the minutes of the meeting or files his written dissent with the secretary of the corporation within two days after the meeting adjourns. A director who has voted in favor of such action shall have no right to such dissent.

ARTICLE IV – OFFICERS

1. NUMBER, ELECTION AND TERM. The corporation shall have the following officers: A president, one or more vice-presidents (the number to be fixed by the board of directors), a secretary, and a treasurer. Each officer shall be elected by the board of directors. Other officers may be elected, appointed or approved by the board. The same person may hold any two or more offices except those of president and secretary. Officers of the corporation to be elected by the board shall be elected annually as soon as convenient after each annual meeting of the shareholders. Each officer shall hold office until a successor has been duly elected, until his death, or until he resigns or has been removed from office by a vote of the board.

2. REMOVAL. Any officer may be removed by the board whenever it believes such removal will serve the best interests of the corporation. A vacancy in any office for any reason may be filled by the board for the unexpired portion of the term.

3. PRESIDENT. The president shall be the principal executive officer of the corporation but shall be subject to the control of the board. The president shall supervise and control all business activities of the corporation. He or his appointed deputy shall preside over all meetings of shareholders and the board. With the secretary or any other officer so authorized by the board, he may sign certificates for shares of the corporation and deeds, mortgages, bonds, contracts, or other instruments which the board has authorized to be executed, except when the board otherwise authorizes or law otherwise requires.

4. VICE-PRESIDENT. In event of the absence, incapacity or death of the president, the vice-president shall perform the duties of the president. When acting as the president, he shall have all the powers of and be subject to all the restrictions upon the president. In general, the vice-president shall perform such duties as the president or board may assign to him.

5. SECRETARY. The secretary shall keep the minutes of the regular and special meetings and other actions of the shareholders and the board; prepare and deliver all notices to comply with any provisions of these by-laws or as required by law; maintain the records and seal of the corporation; keep an up-to-date record of shareholders with address of each shareholder; sign, with the president or vice-president, certificates for shares of the corporation, issued at the direction of the board; and perform all duties as the president or the board may assign to him.

6. TREASURER. The treasurer shall receive all moneys due and payable to the corporation and deposit such moneys in the name of the corporation in the banks or other depositories designated by the board; be responsible for all funds and securities of the corporation; and perform such duties as the president or the board may assign to him.

8. SALARIES. Salaries of officers shall be determined by the board. No officer who receives such salary shall be prevented from also serving as a director of the corporation.

ARTICLE V. CONTRACTS AND BANKING ARRANGEMENTS

1. CONTRACTS. The board may authorize one or more officers or agents to enter into any contract or execute and deliver any instrument in the name of and on behalf of the corporation. The authority thus granted may be general or may be confined to specific circumstances.

2. LOANS. The corporation shall contract no loans or issue any evidences of indebtedness in its name unless a resolution of the board so authorizes.

3. PAYMENT OF CORPORATION FUNDS. All checks, drafts or other orders for the payment of money, notes or other evidences of corporate indebtedness shall be signed only by officers or agents designated by the board.

4. DEPOSITS IN CHECKING AND SAVINGS ACCOUNTS. Funds of the corporation shall be deposited to the credit of the corporation in such banks or savings accounts or invested in such other ways as the board may direct.

ARTICLE VI. CERTIFICATES FOR SHARES AND THEIR TRANSFER

1. CERTIFICATES FOR SHARES. Certificates representing shares of the corporation shall be in the form prescribed by the board. Such certificates shall be signed by the president and secretary and sealed with the corporate seal. Each certificate shall be consecutively numbered. The name and address of the rightful shareholder and the number of shares and date of issue shall be entered on the stock transfer books of the corporation. In case of a transfer of ownership of shares, no new certificate shall be issued until the former certificate for the equivalent number of shares has been surrendered and cancelled. In case of a lost, destroyed or mutilated certificate, a new one may be issued upon such conditions as the board may set down.

2. TRANSFER OF SHARES. Shares of the corporation shall be transferred only on the stock transfer books of the corporation by the holder of record or his legal representative. A request for transfer shall be accompanied by proper evidence of authority to transfer, and on surrender for cancellation of the former certificate for such shares. For all purposes, the

person in whose name shares are registered in the books of the corporation shall be deemed to be their owner.

ARTICLE VII. FISCAL YEAR

The fiscal year of the corporation shall begin on the _____ day of _____ and end on the _____ day of_____ in each year.

ARTICLE VIII. DIVIDENDS

The board may declare and the corporation may pay dividends on its outstanding shares in the manner and upon the terms and conditions provided by law and the Articles of Incorporation of the corporation.

ARTICLE IX. CORPORATE SEAL

The board of directors shall provide a corporate seal. It shall be circular in form and have inscribed on it the name of the corporation, the state of incorporation, and the words "Corporate Seal."

ARTICLE X. WAIVER OF NOTICE

When a notice is required to be given to any shareholder or director of the corporation under the provisions of these by-laws, the provisions of the articles of incorporation or the provisions of the Business Corporation Act of the state of _____ , a waiver in writing signed by the person or persons entitled to such notice, whether before or after the time of the meeting, will be deemed equivalent to the giving of such notice.

ARTICLE XI. STATE LAWS

In any instance in which the by-laws of this corporation conflict with the laws of the state of _____ , the procedures prescribed by statute shall prevail.

Typical Articles of Incorporation
That Meet Requirements of Most States*

1. The name of the corporation is _____
2. The period of its duration is perpetual.
3. Its purpose is to transact the business of _____
   _____ and all other business not
   forbidden by law.
4. It shall have authority to issue _____
   shares, all of one class, _____ par value.
5. The address of its initial registered office is _____
   _____ The name of
   its registered agent at such address is _____
   _____
6. The number of directors constituting its initial board of directors
   is _____ whose names and addresses are:
   _____
   _____
   _____
7. The incorporators are _____
   _____
   _____

                    (Signed) _____
                    _____

                    (Signatures of Incorporators)

Dated _____, 19 ____

*For informational purposes only. Articles of Incorporation should follow
the format prescribed by the State of incorporation.

Minutes, Notices and Proxy Forms
For Meetings of Shareholders and Directors

These minutes, resolutions and forms suggest procedures that may be followed in the conduct of meetings and in recording decisions made and actions taken. No specific style is required in preparing minutes of meetings. However, they should clearly describe all important actions and decisions in order to provide a record if questions concerning a corporate position should arise later.

MINUTES, ORGANIZATION MEETING

The organization meeting of the incorporators of _____ , a corporation, was held at _____ State of _____ on the _____ day of _____, 19 __, at _____ o'clock, ____M.

The following, representing a quorum of incorporators, were present :

_____   _____

_____   _____

_____   _____

The meeting was called to order by _____ .

Motions were duly made, seconded and carried that _____

be elected chairman and that _____ be elected secretary. They accepted the offices and began to discharge their duties.

The secretary read a written waiver of notice of the meeting signed by all the incorporators. The chairman ordered it appended to the minutes of this meeting.

The secretary next brought forward a copy of the certificate of incorporation and reported that the original had been duly filed with the appropriate official of the state of _____ on the _____ day of _____ , 19 __ .

The secretary was instructed to attach to these minutes a copy of the certificate of incorporation and the receipt issued by the state, showing that payment of all the required taxes and filing fees had been made, and confirming the date of the filing of the certificate.

The chairman then proposed that temporary directors be elected.

The following were nominated as directors:

_____   _____

_____   _____

_____   _____

A motion was duly made, seconded and carried, and it was unaminously resolved that each nominee named above be elected a temporary director of the corporation.

A motion was duly made, seconded and carried, and affirmatively voted by all present that the board of directors be authorized to issue all unsubscribed shares of the corporation in such amounts and at such times as the board determines, and to accept in payment money or other property, labor, or other services performed for the corporation or for its benefit.

The chairman next read, article by article and in its entirety, the proposed by-laws for the conduct and regulation of the business and affairs of the corporation.

A motion was duly made, seconded and carried that the proposed by-laws be adopted as the by-laws of this corporation.

The secretary was instructed to insert the by-laws in the minute book.

A motion was duly made, seconded and carried that the principal office of the corporation be fixed at _____,
County of _____, State of _____ .

There was no further business before the meeting. A motion was duly made, seconded and carried that the meeting be adjourned.

Dated the _____ day of _____ 19 ___ .

_____
                                     Secretary

_____
Incorporators   Chairman

Appended hereto:
Waiver of notice of organization meeting
Copy of certificate of incorporation
Receipt of department of state
By-laws

WAIVER OF NOTICE, ORGANIZATION MEETING

We, the undersigned, being the incorporators named in the certificate of incorporation of_____, hereby agree and consent that the organization meeting thereof be held on the date and at the time and place stated below. We hereby waive all notice of the meeting and of any adjournment thereof.

Place of meeting _____
Date and time of meeting _____

                                     _____

                                     _____

Dated: _____   Incorporators

MINUTES, FIRST MEETING OF BOARD OF DIRECTORS

The first meeting of the board of directors of _____
was held at No. _____ , City of _____ ,
State of _____ , on the _____ day of
_____ , 19 ___ , at _____ o'clock ___ M.

The following, representing a quorum of all the directors, were present:

_____ _____

_____ _____

_____ _____

A motion was duly made, seconded and carried that _____
be elected temporary chairman and that _____ be elected
temporary secretary.

The secretary read a waiver of notice of meeting, signed by all the
directors of the corporation. It was ordered made a part of the minutes of the
meeting.

After being duly nominated, the following were unanimously elected to
serve as officers of the corporation for one year:

President _____

Vice President _____

Secretary _____

Treasurer _____

The president and secretary assumed their offices.

A seal was presented to the meeting by the secretary. A motion was duly
made, seconded and carried that this seal, identical to the impression made in
these minutes, be adopted as the official seal of the corporation.

Upon motions duly made, seconded and carried, it was

RESOLVED, that the president and treasurer be authorized to issue, as
certificates for shares of the corporation, the certificates shown to this
meeting and appended to the minutes of the meeting;

RESOLVED, that the share and transfer book to be adopted as the share
and transfer book of the corporation be identical to the share and transfer
book presented at the meeting;

RESOLVED, that the treasurer be authorized to open a checking account
for the purpose of receiving deposits and making withdrawals in the name of
the corporation at the __(Name of Bank)__ in the City of _____ ,
State of _____ , and that withdrawals from this account be made
only by _____ , and _____ , and

_____ .

RESOLVED, that a savings account be opened in the name of the
corporation at the __(Name of Savings Institution)__ in the City of _____ ,
State of _____ , and that withdrawals from this account be made
only by _____ , _____ , and

_____ .

The secretary then presented a written proposal to the corporation from
_____ , to transfer the assets of _____ ,
of which he is the owner, to the corporation as of the _____

day of _____, 19 ___. In consideration of the transfer of such assets, subject to liabilities, he proposes to receive _____ shares of the common stock of the corporation.

The proposal was considered by the board. A motion was duly made, seconded and carried that it be

RESOLVED that said offer, as set forth in the above proposal, represents a fair offer to the corporation and that said offer be approved and accepted. It was further

RESOLVED that the president and treasurer of the corporation be authorized to accept delivery of said assets and to issue to the offerer, in full payment thereof, _____ fully paid and non-assessable shares of this corporation.

The chairman proposed that the corporation adopt a plan for the issuance of its stock. He stated that, in order to qualify the stock under Section 1244 of the Internal Revenue Code, the plan should offer only common stock of the corporation for a specified offering period not to exceed two years from the date of the plan's adoption. After discussion with respect to the proposal, upon motion duly made, seconded and unanimously carried, it was:

RESOLVED, that this corporation adopt and it does hereby adopt the following plan for the offering of only its _____par value common stock (the "stock") intended to qualify under Section 1244 of the Internal Revenue Code:

1. This corporation shall offer the stock to _____ , _____ and _____, (offerees need not be named) or any one or more of them. Upon their acceptance of this offer, it shall sell and issue to them an aggregate of not more than _____ shares of the stock at a price of $ _____per share.

2. The maximum amount to be received by this corporation for the stock offered under this plan shall be $ _____ (cannot exceed $500,000).

3. The stock offered under this plan shall in no event be issued later than two (2) years from the date hereof.

4. This plan shall terminate on the first occuring of the following:

a. Two years from the date hereof; or,

b. The sale and issuance of all of the stock offered under this plan.

5. No additional stock or securities, of any kind, shall be offered by this corporation while this plan is still in effect.

There being no further business, a motion was duly made, seconded and carried that the meeting be adjourned. Dated the _____ day of_____ , 19 ___.

(Signed) _____
Secretary
(Signed) _____
Chairman

Appended hereto:
Seal of Corporation.
Waiver of notice of meeting.

Specimen certificate for shares.

Resolution designating depository of funds.

Proposal to transfer assets of _____ in exchange for _____ shares of the corporation.

MINUTES, FIRST MEETING OF SHAREHOLDERS

The first meeting of the shareholders of _____ was held at _____ on the _____ day of 19 ___ at _____ o'clock, ___M.

The meeting was duly called to order by the president. He stated the purpose of the meeting.

Next, the secretary read the list of shareholders as they appear in the record book of the corporation. He reported the presence of a quorum of shareholders.

Next, the secretary read a waiver of notice of the meeting, signed by all shareholders. On a motion duly made, seconded and carried, the waiver was ordered appended to the minutes of this meeting.

Next, the president asked the secretary to read: (1) the minutes of the organization meeting of the corporation; and (2) the minutes of the first meeting of the board of directors.

A motion was duly made, seconded and carried unanimously that the following resolution be adopted:

WHEREAS, the minutes of the organization meeting of the corporation and the minutes of the first meeting of the board of directors have been read to this meeting, and

WHEREAS, by-laws were adopted and directors and officers were elected at the organization meeting, it is hereby

RESOLVED that this meeting approves and ratifies the election of the said directors and officers of this corporation for the term of _____ years, and approves, ratifies and adopts said by-laws as the by-laws of the corporation. It is further

RESOLVED that all acts taken and decisions made at the organization meeting and the first meeting of the board are approved and ratified. It is further

RESOLVED that signing of these minutes constitutes full ratification by the signatories and waiver of notice of the meeting.

There being no further business, the meeting was adjourned, Dated the _____ day of _____ 19 ___.

_____   Secretary

_____
_____
_____

Directors

Appended hereto:

Waiver of notice of meeting.

WAIVER OF NOTICE, FIRST MEETING OF SHAREHOLDERS

We the undersigned, being the shareholders of the _____ , agree that the first meeting of shareholders be held on the date and at the time and place stated below in order to elect officers and transact such other business as may lawfully come before the meeting. We hereby waive all notice of such meeting and of any adjournment thereof.

Place of meeting _____
Date of meeting _____
Time of meeting _____

Dated: _____   _____
                                                    Shareholders

NOTICE TO SHAREHOLDERS OF ANNUAL MEETING

The Annual Meeting of Shareholders of _____ for the purpose of electing _____ Directors, and transacting such other business as may properly come before the meeting, will be held on the _____ day of _____ , 19 ___, at _____ o'clock, ___ M, at the office of _____ , City of _____ and State of _____ . Transfer books will remain closed from the _____ day of_____ , 19 ___, until the _____ day of _____ , 19 ___ . Dated the _____ day of _____ , 19 ___ . (Signed) _____
                                                    Secretary

PROXY STATEMENT, ANNUAL MEETING

The undersigned hereby appoints _____ or any one or more of them, attorneys with full power of substitution and revocation to each, for and in the name of the undersigned, with all the powers the undersigned would possess if personally present, to vote the Common Stock of the undersigned in _____ at the Annual Meeting of its Stockholders to be held _____ , and at any adjournments thereof, for the following matters:

(1) FOR (   ) AUTHORITY WITHHELD (   ) the fixing of the number of directors at   and the election of directors for the ensuing year as described in the Proxy Statement.

(2) FOR (   ) AGAINST (   ) ratification of the selection of _____ _____ as auditors for the Corporation for the fiscal year ending _____ .

(3) Upon any other matters which may properly come before such meeting or any adjournment thereof.

If not otherwise specified this Proxy will be voted FOR the above proposals.

(Signed)_____

Stockholder

AFFIDAVIT, MAILING OF NOTICE OF ANNUAL MEETING

STATE OF   )
) ss:
COUNTY OF   )

_____ being duly sworn according to law, deposes and says:

I am the Secretary of_____ , and that on the _____ day of the month of _____ , in the year _____, I personally deposited copies of the aforesaid notice in a post-office box in the City of _____, State of_____ .

Each copy of the notice was in a securely sealed and stamped envelope. One copy was addressed to each person whose name appears on the attached list and to respective post-office addresses as shown on the list.

Sworn to before me

this _____ day of

_____ , 19 ___.   (Signed) _____

NOTARY PUBLIC   Secretary

MINUTES, SHAREHOLDERS' ANNUAL MEETING

The Annual Meeting of Shareholders of _____ was held at _____ , State of _____ , on the _____ day of_____, 19 ___, at _____o'clock, ___M.

The president duly called the meeting to order and outlined its purposes.

The secretary next stated that a notice of meeting had been properly served, introducing an affidavit to this effect which was ordered placed on file. (OR: The secretary stated that a waiver of notice of the meeting had been properly signed by the shareholders and it was placed on file.)

The president proposed the immediate election of a chairman. A motion to that effect was duly made and carried.

It being determined that a quorum was present either in person or by proxy, a voice vote of shareholders was taken. _____ was elected chairman of the meeting.

A motion was duly made and carried that the secretary read the minutes of the preceding meeting of shareholders. Upon completion of the reading, a motion was duly made and carried that the minutes be approved as read. (OR: A motion was duly made and carried that a reading of the preceding meeting of shareholders be waived.)

The president then presented his annual report. (Include report.)

A motion was duly made, seconded and carried that the report be received and filed.

The secretary next presented his report. (Include report.)

A motion was duly made, seconded and carried that the report be received and filed.

The treasurer then presented his report. (Include report.)

A motion was duly made, seconded and carried that the report be received and filed.

The chairman said that election of directors of the corporation for the coming year was the next order of business.

The following were nominated as directors:

_____   _____
_____   _____
_____   _____

The chairman then stated that the board had appointed _____
and _____ as inspectors of election and that they would receive and tally the ballots.

Each shareholder was asked to place his vote in a ballot, stating the number of shares voted, and to sign his name.

The inspectors, after completing a tally of the vote, declared that the following votes had been cast:

Names of Nominees	Number of Votes
_____	_____
_____	_____
_____	_____
_____	_____
_____	_____

The chairman then announced that the following persons had been elected directors: _____
_____ .

A motion was duly made, seconded and carried that the inspectors file the report with the clerk of _____ county (when required by law) and with the secretary of the corporation.

There being no further business, a motion was duly made, seconded and carried that the meeting be adjourned.

Dated the _____ day of _____ , 19 _____ .

(Signed) _____
                                                                            Secretary

NOTICE TO DIRECTORS OF REGULAR BOARD MEETING

A meeting of the Board of _____ will be held at the office of the Corporation at _____ , City of _____ ,   State of _____ , on the _____ day of _____ 19 _____ , at _____ o'clock, for the purpose of transacting all such business as may properly come before the same.

Dated the _____ day of _____ 19_____

(Signed) _____
                                                                            Secretary

MINUTES, REGULAR BOARD MEETING

A meeting of the Board was held at _____ on the _____ day of _____ 19 ____ , at _____ o'clock, ____ M.

The president called the meeting to order.

The secretary called the roll. The following directors were present:

_____ _____ _____ _____

The secretary reported that notice of the time and place of holding the meeting had been given to each director by mail in accordance with the by-laws.

A motion was duly made, seconded and carried that the notice be filed.

The president then stated that, a quorum being present, the meeting could transact business.

Minutes of the preceding meeting of the board, held _____ 19 ____ , were read and adopted.

The president presented his report.

A motion was made, seconded and carried that the president's report be filed.

A motion was made, seconded and carried, that _____ be appointed to audit the books of the treasurer before the same are presented to the shareholders.

A motion was duly made and carried that the meeting elect officers for the ensuing year.

The following were thereupon elected by ballot:

President: _____

Vice-President: _____

Secretary: _____

Treasurer: _____

A motion was duly made and carried that salaries of officers be fixed as follows:

Name _____ Salary per year _____
Name _____ Salary per year _____
Name _____ Salary per year _____

There was no further business. The meeting was adjourned.

Dated: _____ 19 ____ (Signed) _____

Secretary

NOTICE, SPECIAL BOARD MEETING

A special meeting of the Board of Directors of _____ will be held at the office of the Corporation at No. _____ , City of _____ , and State of _____ , on the _____ day of _____ , 19 ____ , at ____ o'clock, ____ M, for the purpose of transacting the following business:

_____

_____

(Signed) _____

Secretary

MINUTES, SPECIAL BOARD MEETING

A special meeting of the Board of Directors of _____
was held at _____, City of _____, State of _____
on the _____ day of _____19____, at _____o'clock___ M.

The president called the meeting to order. He instructed the secretary to call the roll of the directors.

The following directors were present: _____ _____
_____

The president said that this meeting was called at the request of _____
_____ to consider _____ .

The secretary read the notice of meeting. He stated that the same was sent to each director as required by the by-laws of the corporation.

A motion was duly made, seconded and carried that the notice be placed upon the minutes.

The following business was then considered and transacted: _____

There were no further items for the board's consideration and the meeting was adjourned.

Dated: _____   (Signed) _____
                                                                            Secretary

CERTIFICATION, CHECKING OR SAVINGS ACCOUNT

I, as ____(Title of Officer)____ of ____(Name of Corporation)____

hereby certify to _____(Name of Institution)_____

that, at a meeting of the Board of Directors duly called and held and at which a quorum was present and voted, there was duly authorized the application for a (checking) (savings) account in _____
and upon the terms and conditions specified. I further certify that the officers of said corporation authorized to make withdrawals from this account are _____ whose title is _____ ,
and _____ , whose title is _____ .
and that I have been duly authorized to make this certification.

In witness whereof, I have hereunto set my hand as such officer of said corporation and affixed the seal of the corporation this _____ day of
_____, 19 ____ .

(Corporate Seal)   _____

Sections of Internal Revenue Code Dealing With Tax-Free Transfers to Corporation

Sec. 351. Transfer to corporation controlled by transferor.
(a) General rule.

No gain or loss shall be recognized if property is transferred to a corporation (including, in the case of transfers made on or before June 30, 1967, an investment company) by one or more persons solely in exchange for stock or securities in such corporation and immediately after the exchange such person or persons are in control (as defined in section 368 (c)) of the corporation. For purposes of this section, stock or securities issued for services shall not be considered as issued in return for property.

(b) Receipt of property.

If subsection (a) would apply to an exchange but for the fact that there is received, in addition to the stock or securities permitted to be received under subsection (a), other property or money, then—

(1) gain (if any) to such recipient shall be recognized, but not in excess of—

(A) the amount of money received, plus

(B) the fair market value of such other property received; and

(2) no loss to such recipient shall be recognized.

(c) Special rule.

In determining control, for purposes of this section, the fact that any corporate transferor distributes part or all of the stock which it receives in the exchange to its shareholders shall not be taken into account.

Sect. 368. (c) Control.

The term "control" means the ownership of stock possessing at least 80 percent of the total combined voting power of all classes of stock entitled to vote and at least 80 percent of the total number of shares of all other classes of stock of the corporation.

Section of Internal Revenue Code Dealing With Losses on Investments in Corporations

SEC. 1244.

(a) **General Rule.**—In the case of an individual, a loss on section 1244 stock issued to such individual or to a partnership which would (but for this section) be treated as a loss from the sale or exchange of a capital asset shall, to the extent provided in this section, be treated as an ordinary loss.

(b) **Maximum Amount for Any Taxable Year.**—For any taxable year the aggregate amount treated by the taxpayer by reason of this section as an ordinary loss shall not exceed—

(1) $50,000, or

(2) $100,000, in the case of a husband and wife filing a joint return for such year under section 6013.

(c) **Section 1244 Stock Defined.**—

(1) **In General.**—For purposes of this section, the term "section 1244 stock" means common stock in a domestic corporation if—

(A) at the time such stock is issued, such corporation was a small business corporation,

(B) such stock was issued by such corporation for money or other property (other than stock and securities), and

(C) such corporation, during the period of its 5 most recent taxable years ending before the date the loss on such stock was sustained, derived more than 50 percent of its aggregate gross receipts from sources other than royalties, rents, dividends, interests, annuities, and sales or exchanges of stocks or securities.

(2) **Rules for application of paragraph (1)(C).**—

(A) Period taken into account with respect to new corporations.—For purposes of paragraph (1)(C), if the corporation has not been in existence for 5 taxable years ending before the date the loss on the stock was sustained, there shall be substituted for such 5-year period—

(i) the period of the corporation's taxable years ending before such date, or

(ii) if the corporation has not been in existence for 1 taxable year ending before such date, the period such corporation has been in existence before such date.

(B) Gross receipts from sales of securities.—For purposes of paragraph (1)(C), gross receipts from the sales or exchanges of stock or securities shall be taken into account only to the extent of gains therefrom.

(C) Nonapplication where deductions exceed gross income.— Paragraph (1)(C) shall not apply with respect to any corporation if, for the period taken into account for purposes of paragraph (1)(C), the amount of the deductions allowed by this chapter (other than by sections 172, 243, 244, and 245) exceeds the amount of gross income.

(3) Small business corporation defined.—

(A) In general.—For purposes of this section, a corporation shall be treated as a small business corporation if the aggregate amount of money and other property received by the corporation for stock, as a contribution to capital, and as paid-in surplus, does not exceed $1,000,000. The determination under the preceding sentence shall be made as of the time of the issuance of the stock in question but shall include amounts received for such stock and for all stock theretofore issued.

(B) Amount taken into account with respect to property.— For purposes of subparagraph (A), the amount taken into account with respect to any property other than money shall be the amount equal to the adjusted basis to the corporation of such property for determining gain, reduced by any liability to which the property was subject or which was assumed by the corporation. The determination under the preceding sentence shall be made as of the time the property was received by the corporation.

(d) Special Rules.—

(1) Limitations on amount of ordinary loss.—

(A) Contributions of property having basis in excess of value.—If—

(i) section 1244 stock was issued in exchange for property,

(ii) the basis of such stock in the hands of the taxpayer is determined by reference to the basis in his hands of such property, and

(iii) the adjusted basis (for determining loss) of such property immediately before the exchange exceeded its fair market value at such time,

then in computing the amount of the loss on such stock for purposes of this section the basis of such stock shall be reduced by an amount equal to the excess described in clause (iii).

(B) Increases in basis.—In computing the amount of the loss on stock for purposes of this section, any increase in the basis of such stock (through contributions to the capital of the corporation, or otherwise) shall be treated as allocable to stock which is not section 1244 stock.

(2) Recapitalizations, changes in name, etc. —To the extent provided in regulations prescribed by the Secretary, common stock in a corporation, the basis of which (in the hands of a taxpayer) is determined in whole or in part by reference to the basis in his hands of stock in such corporation which meets the requirements of subsection (c)(1) (other than subparagraph (C) thereof), or which is received in a reorganization described in section 368(a)(1)(F) in exchange for stock which meets such requirements, shall be treated as meeting such requirements. For purposes of paragraphs (1)(C) and (3)(A) of subsection (c), a successor corporation in a reorganization described in section 368(a)(1)(F) shall be treated as the same corporation as its predecessor.

(3) **Relationship to net operating loss deduction.**—For purposes of section 172 (relating to the net operating loss deduction), any amount of loss treated by reason of this section as an ordinary loss shall be treated as attributable to a trade or business of the taxpayer.

(4) **Individual defined.**— For purposes of this section, the term individual does not include a trust or estate.

(e) **Regulations.**—The Secretary shall prescribe such regulations as may be necessary to carry out the purposes of this section.

Sections of Internal Revenue Code Dealing
With Subchapter S Corporations

SEC. 1371. DEFINITIONS.

(a) **Small Business Corporation.**—For purposes of this subchapter, the term "small business corporation" means a domestic corporation which is not a member of an affiliated group (as defined in section 1504) and which does not—

(1) have more than 15 shareholders;

(2) have as a shareholder a person (other than an estate and other than a trust described in subsection (e)) who is not an individual;

(3) have a nonresident alien as a shareholder; and

(4) have more than one class of stock.

(b) **Electing Small Business Corporation.**— For purposes of this subchapter, the term "electing small business corporation" means, with respect to any taxable year, a small business corporation which has made an election under section 1372(a) which, under section 1372, is in effect for such taxable year.

(c) **Stock Owned by Husband and Wife.** —For purposes of subsection (a)(1), a husband and wife (and their estates) shall be treated as one shareholder.

(d) **Ownership of Certain Stock.** —For purposes of subsection (a), a corporation shall not be considered a member of an affiliated group at any time during any taxable year by reason of the ownership of stock in another corporation if such other corporation—

(1) has not begun business at any time on or after the date of its incorporation and before the close of such taxable year, and

(2) does not have taxable income for the period included within such taxable year.

(e) **Certain Trusts Permitted as Shareholders.** —For purposes of subsection (a), the following trusts may be shareholders:

(1) (A) A trust all of which is treated as owned by the grantor (who is an individual who is a citizen or resident of the United States) under subpart E of part I of subchapter J of this chapter.

(B) A trust which was described in subparagraph (A) immediately before the death of the grantor and which continues in existence after such death, but only for the 60-day period beginning on the day of the grantor's death. If a trust is described in the preceding sentence and if the entire corpus of the trust is includible in the gross estate of the grantor, the preceding sentence shall be applied by substituting "2-year period" for "60-day period."

(2) A trust created primarily to exercise the voting power of stock transferred to it.

(3) Any trust with respect to stock transferred to it pursuant to the terms of a will, but only for the 60-day period beginning on the day on which such stock is transferred to it.

In the case of a trust described in paragraph (1), the grantor shall be treated as the shareholder. In the case of a trust described in paragraph (2), each beneficiary of the trust shall, for purposes of subsection (a)(1), be treated as a shareholder.

SEC. 1372. ELECTION BY SMALL BUSINESS CORPORATION.

(a) **Eligibility**. —Except as provided in subsection (f), any small business corporation may elect, in accordance with the provisions of this section, not to be subject to the taxes imposed by this chapter. Such election shall be valid only if all persons who are shareholders in such corporation on the day on which such election is made consent to such election.

(b) **Effect**. —If a small business corporation makes an election under subsection (a), then—

(1) with respect to the taxable years of the corporation for which such election is in effect, such corporation shall not be subject to the taxes imposed by this chapter (other than as provided by section 58(d)(2) and by section 1378) and, with respect to such taxable years and all succeeding taxable years, the provisions of section 1377 shall apply to such corporation, and

(2) with respect to the taxable years of a shareholder of such corporation in which or with which the taxable years of the corporation for which such election is in effect end, the provisions of sections 1373, 1374, and 1375 shall apply to such shareholder, and with respect to such taxable years and all succeeding taxable years, the provisions of section 1376 shall apply to such shareholder.

(c) **When and How Made.**—

(1) **In General.**—An election under subsection (a) may be made by a small business corporation for any taxable year—

(A) at any time during the preceding taxable year, or

(B) at any time during the first 75 days of the taxable year.

(2) **Treatment of certain late elections.**—If—

(A) a small business corporation makes an election under subsection (a) for any taxable year, and

(B) such election is made after the first 75 days of the taxable year and on or before the last day of such taxable year,

then such election shall be treated as having been made for the following taxable year.

(3) Manner of making election. An election under subsection (a) shall be made in such manner as the Secretary shall prescribe by regulations.

(d) Years for Which Effective. —An election under subsection (a) shall be effective for the taxable year of the corporation for which it is made and for all succeeding taxable years of the corporation, unless it is terminated, with respect to any such taxable year, under subsection (e).

(e) Termination.—

(1) New shareholders.—

(A) An election under subsection (a) made by a small business corporation shall terminate if any person who is not a shareholder in such corporation on the day on which the election is made becomes a shareholder in such corporation and affirmatively refuses (in such manner as the Secretary may by regulations prescribe) to consent to such election on or before the 60th day after the day on which he acquires the stock.

(B) If the person acquiring the stock is the estate of a decedent, the period under subparagraph (A) for affirmatively refusing to consent to the election shall expire on the 60th day after whichever of the following is the earlier:

(i) The day on which the executor or administrator of the estate qualifies, or

(ii) The last day of the taxable year of the corporation in which the decedent died.

(C) Any termination of an election under subparagraph (A) by reason of the affirmative refusal of any person to consent to such election shall be effective for the taxable year of the corporation in which such person becomes a shareholder in the corporation (or, if later, the first taxable year for which such election would otherwise have been effective) and for all succeeding taxable years of the corporation.

(2) Revocation. —An election under subsection (a) made by a small business corporation may be revoked by it for any taxable year of the corporation after the first taxable year for which the election is effective. An election may be revoked only if all persons who are shareholders in the corporation on the day on which the revocation is made consent to ,the revocation. A revocation under this paragraph shall be effective—

(A) for the taxable year in which made, if made before the close of the first month of such taxable year.

(B) for the taxable year following the taxable year in which made, if made after the close of such first month.

and for all succeeding taxable years of the corporation. Such revocation shall be made in such manner as the Secretary shall prescribe by regulations.

(3) Ceases to be small business corporation. —An election under subsection (a) made by a small business corporation shall terminate if at any time—

(A) after the first day of the first taxable year of the corporation for which the election is effective, if such election is made on or before such first day, or

(B) after the day on which the election is made, if such election is made after such first day,

the corporation ceases to be a small business corporation (as defined in section 1371(a)). Such termination shall be effective for the taxable year of the corporation in which the corporation ceases to be a small business corporation and for all succeeding taxable years of the corporation.

(4) **Foreign income.** —An election under subsection (a) made by a small business corporation shall terminate if for any taxable year of the corporation for which the election is in effect, such corporation derives more than 80 percent of its gross receipts from sources outside the United States. Such termination shall be effective for the taxable year of the corporation in which it derives more than 80 percent of its gross receipts from sources outside the United States, and for all succeeding taxable years of the corporation.

(5) **Passive investment income.**—

(A) Except as provided in subparagraph (B), an election under subsection (a) made by a small business corporation shall terminate if, for any taxable year of the corporation for which the election is in effect, such corporation has gross receipts more than 20 percent of which is passive investment income. Such termination shall be effective for the taxable year of the corporation in which it has gross receipts of such amount, and for all succeeding taxable years of the corporation.

(B) Subparagraph (A) shall not apply with respect to a taxable year in which a small business corporation has gross receipts more than 20 percent of which is passive investment income, if—

(i) such taxable year is the first taxable year in which the corporation commenced the active conduct of any trade or business or the next succeeding taxable year; and

(ii) the amount of passive investment income for such taxable year is less than $3,000.

(C) For purposes of this paragraph, the term "passive investment income" means gross receipts derived from royalties, rents, dividends, interest, annuities, and sales or exchanges of stock or securities (gross receipts from such sales or exchanges being taken into account for purposes of this paragraph only to the extent of gains therefrom). Gross receipts derived from sales or exchanges of stock or securities for purposes of this paragraph shall not include amounts received by an electing small business corporation which are treated under section 331 (relating to corporate liquidations) as payments in exchange for stock where the electing small business corporation owned more than 50 percent of each class of the stock of the liquidating corporation.

(f) **Election After Termination.** —If a small business corporation has made an election under subsection (a) and if such election has been terminated or revoked under subsection (e), such corporation (and any successor corporation) shall not be eligible to make an election under subsection (a) for any taxable year prior to its fifth taxable year which begins after the first taxable year for which such termination or revocation is effective, unless the Secretary consents to such election.

(g) [Repealed]

SEC. 1373. CORPORATION UNDISTRIBUTED TAXABLE INCOME TAXED TO SHAREHOLDERS.

(a) **General Rule.** —The undistributed taxable income of an electing small business corporation for any taxable year shall be included in the gross income of the shareholders of such corporation in the manner and to the extent set forth in this section.

(b) **Amount Included in Gross Income.** —Each person who is a shareholder of an electing small business corporation on the last day of a taxable year of such corporation shall include in his gross income, for his taxable year in which or with which the taxable year of the corporation ends, the amount he would have received as a dividend, if on such last day there had been distributed pro rata to its shareholders by such corporation an amount equal to the corporation's undistributed taxable income for the corporation's taxable year. For purposes of this chapter, the amount so included shall be treated as an amount distributed as a dividend on the last day of the taxable year of the corporation.

(c) **Undistributed Taxable Income Defined.** —For purposes of this section, the term "undistributed taxable income" means taxable income (computed as provided in subsection (d)) minus the sum of (1) the taxes imposed by sections 56 and 1378(a) and (2) the amount of money distributed as dividends during the taxable year, to the extent that any such amount is a distribution out of earnings and profits of the taxable year as specified in section 316(a)(2).

(d) **Taxable Income.** —For purposes of this subchapter, the taxable income of an electing small business corporation shall be determined without regard to—

(1) the deduction allowed by section 172 (relating to net operating loss deduction), and

(2) the deductions allowed by part VIII of subchapter B (other than the deduction allowed by section 248, relating to organization expenditures).

SEC. 1374. CORPORATION NET OPERATING LOSS ALLOWED TO SHAREHOLDERS.

(a) **General Rule.** —A net operating loss of an electing small busines corporation for any taxable year shall be allowed as a deduction from gross income of the shareholders of such corporation in the manner and to the extent set forth in this section.

(b) **Allowance of Deduction.** —Each person who is a shareholder of an electing small business corporation at any time during a taxable year of the corporation in which it has a net operating loss shall be allowed as a deduction from gross income, for his taxable year in which or with which the taxable year of the corporation ends (or for the final taxable taxable year of a shareholder who dies before the end of the corporation's taxable year), an amount equal to his portion of the corporation's net operating loss (as determined under subsection (c)). The deduction allowed by this subsection shall, for purposes of this chapter, be considered as a deduction attributable to a trade or business carried on by the shareholder.

(c) **Determination of Shareholder's Portion.**—

(1) **In general.** —For purposes of this section, a shareholder's portion of the net operating loss of an electing small business corporation is his pro rata share of the corporation's net operating loss (computed as provided in section 172(c), except that the deductions provided in part VIII (except section 248) of subchapter B shall not be allowed) for his taxable year in which or with which the taxable year of the corporation ends. For purposes of this paragraph, a shareholder's pro rata share of the corporation's net operating loss is the sum of the portions of the corporation's daily net operating loss attributable on a pro rata basis to the shares held by him on each day of the taxable year. For purposes of the preceding sentence, the corporation's daily net operating loss is the corporation's net operating loss divided by the number of days in the taxable year.

(2) **Limitation.** —A shareholder's portion of the net operating loss of an electing small business corporation for any taxable year shall not exceed the sum of—

(A) the adjusted basis (determined without regard to any adjustment under section 1376 for the taxable year) of the shareholder's stock in the electing small business corporation, determined as of the close of the taxable year of the corporation (or, in respect of stock sold or otherwise disposed of during such taxable year, as of the day before the day of such sale or other disposition), and

(B) the adjusted basis (determined without regard to any adjustment under section 1376 for the taxable year) of any indebtedness of the corporation to the shareholder, determined as of the close of the taxable year of the corporation (or, if the shareholder is not a shareholder as of the close of such taxable year, as of the close of the last day in such taxable year on which the shareholder was a shareholder in the corporation).

SEC. 1375. SPECIAL RULES APPLICABLE TO DISTRIBUTIONS OF ELECTING SMALL BUSINESS CORPORATIONS.

(a) **Capital Gains.**—

(1) **Treatment in hands of shareholders.** —The amount includible in the gross income of a shareholder as dividends (including amounts treated as dividends under section 1373(b)) from an electing small business corporation during any taxable year of the corporation, to the extent that such amount is a distribution of property out of earnings and profits of the taxable year as specified in section 316(a)(2), shall be treated as a long-term capital gain to the extent of the shareholder's pro

rata share of the corporation's net capital gain for such taxable year. For purposes of this paragraph, such net capital gain shall be deemed not to exceed the corporation's taxable income (computed as provided in section 1373(d)) for the taxable year.

(2) **Determination of shareholder's pro rata share.** —A shareholder's pro rata share of such gain for any taxable year shall be an amount which bears the same ratio to such gain as the amount of dividends described in paragraph (1) includible in the shareholder's gross income bears to the entire amount of dividends described in paragraph (1) includible in the gross income of all shareholders.

(3) **Reduction for taxes imposed.** For purposes of paragraphs (1) and (2), an electing small business corporation's net capital gain for a taxable year shall be reduced by an amount equal to the amount of the taxes imposed by sections 56 and 1378(a) on such corporation for such year.

(b) **Dividends Not Treated as Such for Certain Purposes.** —The amount includible in the gross income of a shareholder as dividends from an electing small business corporation during any taxable year of the corporation (including any amount treated as a dividend under section 1373(b)) shall not be considered as a dividend for purposes of section 37 or section 116 to the extent that such amount is a distribution of property out of earnings and profits of the taxable year as specified in section 316(a)(2). For purposes of this subsection, the earnings and profits of the taxable year shall be deemed not to exceed the corporation's taxable income (computed as provided in section 1373(d) for the taxable year.

(c) **Treatment of Family Groups.** —Any dividend received by a shareholder from an electing small business corporation (including any amount treated as a dividend under section 1373(b)) may be apportioned or allocated by the Secretary between or among shareholders of such corporation who are members of such shareholder's family (as defined in section 704(e)(3)), if he determines that such apportionment or allocation is necessary in order to reflect the value of services rendered to the corporation by such shareholders.

(d) **Distributions of Undistributed Taxable Income Previously Taxed to Shareholders.**—

(1) **Distributions not considered as dividends.** —An electing small business corporation may distribute, in accordance with regulations prescribed by the Secretary, to any shareholder all or any portion of the shareholder's net share of the corporation's undistributed taxable income for taxable years prior to the taxable year in which such distribution is made. Any such distribution shall, for purposes of this chapter, be considered a distribution which is not a dividend, but the earnings and profits of the corporation shall not be reduced by reason of any such distribution.

(2) **Shareholder's net share of undistributed taxable income.** —For purposes of this subsection, a shareholder's net share of the undistributed taxable income of an electing small business corporation is an amount equal to—

(A) the sum of the amounts included in the gross income of the

shareholder under section 1373(b) for all prior taxable years (excluding any taxable year to which the provisions of this section do not apply and all taxable years preceding such year), reduced by
    (B) the sum of—
        (i) the amounts allowable under section 1374(b) as a deduction from gross income of the shareholder for all prior taxable years (excluding any taxable year to which the provisions of this section do not apply and all taxable years preceding such year), and
        (ii) all amounts previously distributed during the taxable year and all prior taxable years (excluding any taxable year to which the provisions of this section do not apply and all taxable years preceding such year) to the shareholder which under subsection (f) or paragraph (1) of this subsection were considered distributions which were not dividends.

(e) [Repealed]

(f) **Distributions Within 2½-Month Period After Close of Taxable Year.**—

(1) **Distributions considered as distributions of undistributed taxable income.**— Any distribution of money made by a corporation after the close of a taxable year with respect to which it was an electing small business corporation and on or before the 15th day of the third month following the close of such taxable year to a person who was a shareholder of such corporation at the close of such taxable year shall be treated as a distribution of the corporation's undistributed taxable income for such year, to the extent such distribution (when added to the sum of all prior distributions of money made to such person by such corporation following the close of such year) does not exceed such person's share of the corporation's undistributed taxable income for such year. Any distribution so treated shall, for purposes of this chapter, be considered a distribution which is not a dividend, and the earnings and profits of the corporation shall not be reduced by reason of such distribution.

(2) **Share of undistributed taxable income.** —For purposes of paragraph (1), a person's share of a corporation's undistributed taxable income for a taxable year is the amount required to be included in his gross income under section 1373(b) as a shareholder of such corporation for his taxable year in which or with which the taxable year of the corporation ends.

SEC. 1376. ADJUSTMENT TO BASIS OF STOCK OF, AND INDEBTEDNESS OWING, SHAREHOLDERS.

(a) **Increase in Basis of Stock for Amounts Treated as Dividends.** —The basis of a shareholder's stock in an electing small business corporation shall be increased by the amount required to be included in the gross income of such shareholder under section 1373(b), but only to the extent to which such amount is included in his gross income in his return, increased or decreased by any adjustment of such amount in any redetermination of the shareholder's tax liability.

(b) Reduction in Basis of Stock and Indebtedness for Shareholder's Portion of Corporation Net Operating Losses.—

(1) Reduction in basis of stock. —The basis of a shareholder's stock in an electing small business corporation shall be reduced (but not below zero) by an amount equal to the amount of his portion of the corporation's net operating loss for any taxable year attributable to such stock (as determined under section 1374(c)).

(2) Reduction in basis of indebtedness. —The basis of any indebtedness of an electing small business corporation to a shareholder of such corporation shall be reduced (but not below zero) by an amount equal to the amount of the shareholder's portion of the corporation's net operating loss for any taxable year (as determined under section 1374(c)), but only to the extent that such amount exceeds the adjusted basis of the stock of such corporation held by the shareholder.

SEC. 1377. SPECIAL RULES APPLICABLE TO EARNINGS AND PROFITS OF ELECTING SMALL BUSINESS CORPORATIONS.

(a) Reduction for Undistributed Taxable Income. —The accumulated earnings and profits of an electing small business corporation as of the close of its taxable year shall be reduced to the extent that its undistributed taxable income for such year is required to be included in the gross income of the shareholder of such corporation under section 1373(b).

(b) Current Earnings and Profits Not Reduced by Any Amount Not Allowable as Deduction. —The earnings and profits of an electing small business corporation for any taxable year (but not its accumulated earnings and profits) shall not be reduced by any amount which is not allowable as a deduction in computing its taxable income (as provided in section 1373(d)) for such taxable year.

(c) Earnings and Profits Not Affected by Net Operating Loss. —The earnings and profits and the accumulated earnings and profits of an electing small business corporation shall not be affected by any item of gross income or any deduction taken into account in determining the amount of any net operating loss (computed as provided in section 1374(c)) of such corporation.

(d) Distributions of Undistributed Taxable Income Previously Taxed to Shareholders. —For purposes of determining whether a distribution by an electing small business corporation constitutes a distribution of such corporation's undistributed taxable income previously taxed to shareholders (as provided for in section 1375(d)), the earnings and profits of such corporation for the taxable year in which the distribution is made shall be computed without regard to section 312(k). Such computation shall be made without regard to section 312(k) only for such purposes.

SEC. 1378. TAX IMPOSED ON CERTAIN CAPITAL GAINS.

(a) General Rule. —If for a taxable year of an electing small business corporation—

(1) the net capital gain of such corporation exceeds $25,000, and exceeds 50 percent of its taxable income for such year, and

(2) the taxable income of such corporation for such year exceeds $25,000,

there is hereby imposed a tax (computed under subsection (b)) on the income of such corporation.

(b) **Amount of Tax.** —The tax imposed by subsection (a) shall be the lower of—

(1) an amount equal to the tax, determined as provided in section 1201(a), on the amount by which the net capital gain of the corporation for taxable year exceeds $25,000, or

(2) an amount equal to the tax which would be imposed by section 11 on the taxable income (computed as provided in section 1373(d)) of the corporation for the taxable year if the corporation was not an electing small business corporation.

No credit shall be allowable under part IV of subchapter A of this chapter (other than under section 39) against the tax imposed by subsection (a).

(c) **Exceptions.**—

(1) **In general.**—Subsection (a) shall not apply to an electing small business corporation for any taxable year if the election under section 1372(a) which is in effect with respect to such corporation for such taxable year has been in effect for the 3 immediately preceding taxable years.

(2) **New corporations.**—Subsection (a) shall not apply to an electing small business corporation if—

(A) it has been in existence for less than 4 taxable years, and

(B) an election under section 1372(a) has been in effect with respect to such corporation for each of its taxable years.

(3) **Property with substituted basis.** —If—

(A) but for paragraph (1) or (2), subsection (a) would apply for the taxable year,

(B) any long-term capital gain is attributable to property acquired by the electing small business corporation during the period beginning 3 years before the first day of the taxable year and ending on the last day of the taxable year, and

(C) the basis of such property is determined in whole or in part by reference to the basis of any property in the hands of another corporation which was not an electing small busines corporation throughout all of the period described in subparagraph (B) before the transfer by such other corporation and during which such other corporation was in existence,

then subsection (a) shall apply for the taxable year, but the amount of the tax determined under subsection (b) shall not exceed a tax, determined as provided in section 1201(a), on the net capital gain attributable to property acquired as provided in subparagraph (B) and having a basis described in subparagraph (C).

SEC. 1379. CERTAIN QUALIFIED PENSION, ETC., PLANS.

(a) **Additional Requirement for Qualification of Stock Bonus or Profit-Sharing Plans.** —A trust forming part of a stock bonus or profit-sharing plan which provides contributions or benefits for employees some or all of whom are shareholder-employees shall not constitute a qualified trust under section 401 (relating to qualified pension, profit-sharing, and stock bonus plans) unless the plan of which such trust is a part provides that forfeitures attributable to contributions deductible under section 404(a)(3) for any taxable year (beginning after December 31, 1970) of the employer with respect to which it is an electing small business corporation may not inure to the benefit of any individual who is a shareholder-employee for such taxable year. A plan shall be considered as satisfying the requirement of this subsection for the period beginning with the first day of a taxable year and ending with the 15th day of the third month following the close of such taxable year, if all the provisions of the plan which are necessary to satisfy this requirement are in effect by the end of such period and have been made effective for all purposes with respect to the whole of such period.

(b) **Taxability of Shareholder-Employee Beneficiaries.**—

(1) **Inclusion of excess contributions in gross income.**—Notwithstanding the provisions of section 402 (relating to taxability of beneficiary of employees' trust), section 403 (relating to taxation of employee annuities), or section 405(d) (relating to taxability of beneficiaries under qualified bond purchase plans), an individual who is a shareholder-employee of an electing small business corporation shall include in gross income, for his taxable year in which or with which the taxable year of the corporation ends, the excess of the amount of contributions paid on his behalf which is deductible under section 404(a)(1), (2), or (3) by the corporation for its taxable year over the lesser of—

(A) 15 percent of the compensation received or accrued by him from such corporation during its taxable year, or
(B) $7,500.

(2) **Treatment of amounts included in gross income.** — Any amount included in the gross income of a shareholder-employee under paragraph (1) shall be treated as consideration for the contract contributed by the shareholder-employee for purposes of Section 72 (relating to annuities).

(3) **Deduction for amounts not received as benefits.** —If—

(A) amounts are included in the gross income of an individual under paragraph (1), and
(B) the rights of such individual (or his beneficiaries) under the plan terminate before payments under the plan which are excluded from gross income equal the amounts included in gross income under paragraph (1).

then there shall be allowed as a deduction, for the taxable year in which such rights terminate, an amount equal to the excess of the amounts included in gross income under paragraph (1) over such payments.

(c) **Carryover of Amounts Deductible.** —No amount deductible shall be carried forward under the second sentence of section 404(a)(3)(A) (relating to limits on deductible contributions under stock bonus and profit-sharing trusts) to a taxable year of a corporation with respect to which it is not an electing small business corporation from a taxable year (beginning after December 31, 1970) with respect to which it is an electing small business corporation.

(d) **Shareholder-Employee.** —For purposes of this section, the term "shareholder-employee" means an employee or officer of an electing small business corporation who owns (or is considered as owning within the meaning of section 318(a)(1)), on any day during the taxable year of such corporation, more than 5 percent of the outstanding stock of the corporation.

Index